EFFICIENT
CAPITAL MARKETS
AND ACCOUNTING

Prentice-Hall

Contemporary Topics in Accounting Series

ALFRED RAPPAPORT, SERIES EDITOR

BEAVER, *Financial Reporting: An Accounting Revolution*

DYCKMAN and MORSE, *Efficient Capital Markets and Accounting: A Critical Analysis, second edition*

HOPWOOD, *Accounting and Human Behavior*

LEV, *Financial Statement Analysis: A New Approach*

LIBBY, *Accounting and Human Information Processing: Theory and Applications*

REVSINE, *Replacement Cost Accounting*

WATTS and ZIMMERMAN, *Positive Accounting Theory*

EFFICIENT CAPITAL MARKETS AND ACCOUNTING:

A CRITICAL ANALYSIS

Second Edition

THOMAS R. DYCKMAN
Cornell University

DALE MORSE
Cornell University

PRENTICE-HALL, INC., ENGLEWOOD CLIFFS, NEW JERSEY 07632

225801

Library of Congress Cataloging in Publication Data
DYCKMAN, THOMAS R.
  Efficient capital markets and accounting.

  (Contemporary topics in accounting series)
  Bibliography: p. 92.
  Includes index.
  1. Efficient market theory. 2. Stocks—Prices—
United States. 3. Corporations—United States—
Accounting. I. Morse, Dale (date). II. Title.
III. Series.
HG4915.D95 1986   658.1'52   84-26630
ISBN 0-13-246992-8

Editorial/production supervision: Joan Foley
Manufacturing buyer: Ray Keating

Printed in the United States of America

10 9 8 7 6 5 4 3 2

ISBN 0-13-246992-8 01

Prentice-Hall International (UK) Limited, *London*
Prentice-Hall of Australia Pty. Limited, *Sydney*
Editora Prentice-Hall do Brasil, Ltda., *Rio de Janeiro*
Prentice-Hall Canada Inc., *Toronto*
Prentice-Hall Hispanoamericana, S.A., *Mexico*
Prentice-Hall of India Private Limited, *New Delhi*
Prentice-Hall of Japan, Inc., *Tokyo*
Prentice-Hall of Southeast Asia Pte. Ltd., *Singapore*
Whitehall Books Limited, *Wellington, New Zealand*

Dedicated to

Professor William Beaver
Stanford University

Contents

Foreword

Accounting, broadly conceived as the measurement and communication of economic information relevant to decision makers, has undergone dramatic changes during the past decade. Recent advances in quantitative methods, the behavioral sciences, and information technology are influencing current thinking in financial as well as managerial accounting. Leasing, pension plans, the use of convertible securities and warrants in mergers and acquisitions, inflation, and corporate diversification are but a few of the challenging problems facing the accountant.

These developments and the very pervasiveness of accounting activity make it difficult for teachers, students, public accountants, and financial executives to gain convenient access to current thinking on key topics in the field. Journal articles, while current, must often of necessity give only cursory treatment or present a single point of view. Many of the important developments in the field have not crystalized to a point where they can be easily incorporated into textbooks. Further, because textbooks must necessarily limit the space devoted to any one topic, key topics often do not get the attention they properly deserve.

The Contemporary Topics series attempts to fill this gap by covering significant contemporary developments in accounting through brief, but self-contained, studies. These independent studies provide the reader with up-to-date coverage of key topics. For the practitioner, the series offers a succinct overview of developments in research and practice in areas of special interest to him. The series enables the teacher to design courses with maximum flexibility and to expose his students to authoritative analysis of controversial problems.

ALFRED RAPPAPORT

Preface

Since the completion of the first edition of this book in 1974, market efficiency has become a common part of the terminology used in the investment world. In an efficient market, security prices accurately reflect information, and investors cannot use this information to obtain consistently higher returns than justified by an investment's risk. These ideas are known as the efficient market hypothesis (EMH). Although knowledge of the EMH has become widespread, it still has not been generally accepted as a basis for making investment decisions. Therefore, the questions addressed in the first edition are still relevant today.

Are securities markets efficient? What are the implications of the EMH for accounting? Does accounting have a role if markets are efficient? What should be the role of the Securities and Exchange Commission and the Financial Accounting Standards Board in regulating accounting practices? What are the implications of market efficiency for accounting research?

A considerable amount of attention has been given to these questions by scholars since the previous edition of this book. Earlier answers to these questions have been modified in light of their efforts. This book summarizes this research and analyzes the results in terms of the effect on accounting policy, practice, and research.

The quantity and focus of recent research has necessitated a change in the format of this edition. When the previous edition was written, only a limited number of articles related to the EMH. These articles were primarily empirical and focused on the experimental and statistical methodology used to test the EMH. As a result, the original edition examined the experimental procedures in great detail. Subsequent research, however, has demonstrated that many of the results are not sensitive to the experimental procedures. Tests are commonly performed using a variety of procedures without having a significant impact on the results. Therefore, in this edition of the book less space is devoted to procedural issues.

Questions about the meaning of market efficiency and the testability of the EMH in conjunction with a pricing model have replaced procedural issues. What is meant by market efficiency? How is market efficiency related to rationality and market equilibrium? Are attempts to test the EMH really tests of the pricing model? Can these tests tell us something about how securities are priced? These issues are the focus of the new edition.

Because of the large quantity of literature that has recently been published on the EMH, this survey is limited to research using the New York Stock Exchange and, in some cases, the American Stock Exchange as a data base. Many studies have also been made on foreign, bond, and other types of markets. These studies are not reviewed.

With a few exceptions, our survey is further limited to articles that have made some attempt to adjust returns for risk. This restriction eliminates most studies before 1968. However, some of these studies have since been replicated using risk-adjusted returns.

Finally, most of the articles reviewed are published in academic journals. Working papers are often difficult to obtain and have not gone through a rigorous review. In some cases, however, working papers that provide a valuable topical link are referenced. But even these limitations do not explain all the articles on the EMH not covered here. In some cases, for the sake of brevity, representative papers from certain areas have been chosen. We apologize to authors who feel that their work is erroneously omitted or misinterpreted. The final conclusions are ours, but they have been molded by the research of our colleagues in accounting, economics, and finance.

CHAPTER ONE

The Efficient Market Hypothesis

In a competitive market, the equilibrium price of any good or service at a particular moment is such that the available supply is equated to the aggregate demand. This price represents a consensus of the members trading in the market about the worth of the good or service, based on all publicly available information. As soon as a new piece of relevant information becomes available, it is analyzed and interpreted by the market. The result is a possible change in the existing equilibrium price. The new equilibrium price holds until yet another bit of information is available for analysis and interpretation. For example, the performance of some companies is considered to be heavily dependent on the effectiveness of the chief executive officer. If that individual should suddenly leave the firm, the announcement could lead to a fall in the company's stock price, especially if there is no obvious successor who can take over.

The purpose of this book is to examine recent evidence on how stock prices adjust to new information. The primary hypothesis is that stock prices accurately reflect available information. If so, no amount of security analysis can consistently yield above-normal returns, and stock prices will adjust rapidly and appropriately to new information. This hypothesis is known as the *efficient market hypothesis (EMH)*. The EMH is sufficiently general to cover markets

1

other than the securities markets, including those for real estate, antiques, paintings, and others. Our concern, however, is with the markets for securities.

A discussion of attempts at more precise definitions of market efficiency is provided in Chapter 2. But for the purpose of this chapter and the review of empirical work in subsequent chapters, market efficiency refers to the rapidity and accuracy of price adjustments to new information. Both the speed and accuracy of adjustment are conceptually continuous measures. Those markets that adjust more rapidly and accurately to information are considered more efficient. Although market efficiency is sometimes referred to in absolute terms, instantaneous price adjustment is impossible because trading does not occur continuously in securities markets. For purposes of this book, a market is considered efficient if an investor, with normal access to the market, cannot take advantage of any delays in price adjustments reflecting new information.

The alternative hypothesis is that security markets are not efficient. The primary argument for this hypothesis is based on the inability of investors to interpret new information. For example, a change in accounting methods, it is argued, may cause confusion among investors. The result of this confusion would then lead to prices not reflecting the information. Another potential cause of prices failing to reflect information is the incomplete dissemination of information. If some investors don't have the information, the argument maintains, their demand, and possibly prices, could be affected. Further, constraints in the market may also affect prices. Transaction costs in buying and selling securities and restrictions on short sales may inhibit prices from reflecting new information.

Testing the EMH is difficult because whether security prices are correct cannot be directly observed. Most tests of market efficiency examine the ability of information-based trading strategies to make above-normal returns. A trading strategy that would consistently realize above-normal returns is not consistent with the EMH. To test for above-normal returns, however, the normal or expected return must first be defined. Several models describing expected returns are used. The most common model is the *capital asset pricing model (CAPM)*, even though many researchers now question its adequacy. Given general disagreement about which pricing model should be used to determine expected returns, testing the EMH is difficult if not impossible.

Because of the difficulty of testing the EMH, market efficiency, like rationality, is often simply assumed in recent studies. Assuming market efficiency allows the researcher to focus on the question of how securities are priced. The CAPM is a simplistic approach to pricing securities and is not likely to be completely accurate. By studying the relationship between information and security prices, more comprehensive pricing models will be derived.

1.1 ACCOUNTING INFORMATION AND SECURITIES MARKETS

Securities are claims on the assets of the issuing organization. Yet securities differ with respect to the rights granted to the holder. Holders of debt generally have claims to a specified amount of assets at certain dates. Holders of common stock, on the other hand, maintain voting rights but only a residual claim on assets following payments to debtholders. Studies of the EMH have focused almost entirely on the markets for common stock.

Common stock markets have certain characteristics that are likely to make them more efficient than most other markets. Hence, common stock markets provide a reasonable place to begin the analysis. If these markets are not efficient, it is unlikely that other markets will be efficient.

Common stocks are traded on organized exchanges, including the New York Stock Exchange (NYSE) and the American Stock Exchange (AMEX), or in dealer markets such as the over-the-counter (OTC) markets. Both organized and dealer markets allow a rapid execution of buy and sell orders. Therefore, the price response to any change in demand caused by new information can occur in a very short time period.

Common stock markets are also competitive due to the large number of participating individuals, institutions, corporations, and other traders. These participants use available information to make investment decisions with the objective of increasing their wealth. The competitive forces in the stock markets tend to cause prices to reflect the available information quickly. A market that quickly and accurately reflects available information is known as an efficient market.

The distribution system of information about corporations also contributes to creating an efficient market. A number of legal restrictions exist in combination with the usual competitive pressures and moral obligations that motivate corporate managers and other insiders not to be selective in their dissemination of information. The existence of a large and well-established brokerage industry, an independent financial press, and a rapid and extensive communications system further assist in complete retrieval, analysis, interpretation, and distribution of corporate information.

The most publicized information sources on corporations are their interim and annual accounting statements. The issuance and form of these reports are regulated by the Securities and Exchange Commission (SEC) based on reporting principles established by the Financial Accounting Standards Board (FASB). These reports are used by both amateur and professional investors in conjunction with other information to predict a firm's future performance and thereby provide a base for estimating future stock prices and the related cash flows to investors.

The inability to assess correctly the implications of information may occur when new types of information arrive in the market. For example, the implications of the oil embargo on stock prices were difficult to assess because the event was quite unusual. Learning will have occurred, however, so if another oil embargo occurs, prices should adjust more rapidly than before. As similar or even related information events become repetitious, learning takes place and the market becomes more efficient.

The arguments just presented are based on information processing costs. The market may also be inefficient because information is costly to obtain. Information acquired from private sources may only be purchased by a portion of the investors. Also, information that is released to the public through media such as *The Wall Street Journal* may reach some investors at a later time period and other investors not at all. Therefore, even information that is treated in studies as publicly available may not be received by all investors. The effect of uninformed investors may cause prices not to adjust completely or rapidly to the information.

There are in addition several factors related to the operation of stock markets that create the potential for stocks to be mispriced given available information. Not all investors have immediate access to the market, so that price reactions to new information may be delayed until these investors have submitted revised demands based on the new information. Also, there are transaction costs (e.g., brokerage fees) that may inhibit the flow of funds in the stock market. Restrictions on short selling limit the influence of investors with negative beliefs about securities. Also, dealers and specialists cause price fluctuations that reflect bid-ask spreads rather than new information. The effects of these market imperfections on prices are uncertain, but they have the potential for causing prices to deviate from prices that fully reflect available information.

1.2 THE EFFICIENT MARKET HYPOTHESIS

The EMH maintains that the total market is quite sophisticated in the way in which it digests financial statement data and arrives at equilibrium security prices. Furthermore, equilibrium occurs in spite of the unsophisticated (or naïve) nature of many, if not most, of the individuals who, collectively in number, make up the market. A securities market is generally defined as efficient if (1) the prices of the securities traded in the market act as though they fully reflect all available information and (2) these prices react instantaneously, or nearly so, and in an unbiased fashion to new information. Although this definition is sufficient for our immediate purposes, a more detailed discussion is presented in Chapter 2.

The ability of the market price to adjust quickly and accurately to information derives from the existence of a group of professional investors who are capable of gathering, analyzing, and interpreting all types of information on the companies whose securities are being traded. Through constant and careful attention to the market and because of the large volume and frequency with which they trade, these professionals ensure that prices are set competitively, and the prices quickly (if not instantaneously) impound new information. In this type of market, investors who misinterpret information have little, if any, influence on prices.

Fama [1970] coined the phrase "efficient market" to describe a market with prices that fully reflect information. He further categorized different levels of market efficiency (the weak, semistrong, and strong forms) based on the type of information involved. *Weak-form market efficiency* occurs when prices reflect all the information embodied in the past price series. Markets are efficient in *the semistrong form* when prices reflect all publicly available information. *Strong-form* market efficiency occurs when prices reflect all information, both public and private. Strong-form market efficiency implies semistrong-form market efficiency, and semistrong-form market efficiency in turn implies weak-form market efficiency.

1.2.1 Weak-Form Market Efficiency

Studies of weak-form market efficiency began long before market efficiency was defined. Studies of the ability of past prices to predict future prices began with Louis Bachelier [1900], who studied commodity prices in France and concluded that the current price of a commodity was also an unbiased estimate of its future price. This is consistent with the statistical definition of a random walk as applied to the series of commodity prices, although Bachelier did not use that term. (A *random walk* is a time series with the expected value in the next period equal to the most recent value. Other past elements of the time series provide no information about the expected value next period.) It was another 60 years before further research on security prices again suggested the hypothesis that stock prices followed a random walk. Two studies published in 1959 suggested that price changes were independent of each other. A paper by Roberts [1959] simply showed that a series of numbers following a random walk look very much like a series of stock prices; a study by Osborne [1959] found the movement of stock prices similar to that of the movement of small particles suspended in a chemical solution. These studies ushered in a boom of research interest on this topic. Studies by Granger and Morgenstern [1963], Moore [1964], and Fama [1965], which are discussed in more detail in Chapter 3, provided support for the tentative findings of Roberts and Osborne. Collectively, this work served to convince many academics, and even a few practitioners, that security prices did indeed follow a random walk. The argument that stock price changes are random does not mean that such changes take place without cause or reason. On the contrary, prices change because of changes in the perceived earnings potential of the issuing firm or changes in the returns expected from alternative investments. In other words, the set of knowledge on a specific security is frequently revised and updated, leading to changes in the security's price. The *random walk hypothesis* simply states that at a given point in time, the size and direction of the next price change is random with respect to the knowledge available at that point in time.

The finding that investors are unable to forecast future prices by studying only the series of past prices is evidence supporting the weak form of efficient market hypothesis. This result suggests that charting and other forms of technical analysis practiced by many investors, amateur and professional alike, are of questionable value.

1.2.2 Semistrong-Form Market Efficiency

To assert that markets are efficient in the semistrong sense, the researcher must demonstrate that current prices reflect not only the information contained in the sequence of past prices but all publicly available information on the firm whose securities are being traded. This implies that the market prices of securities adjust rapidly and in an unbiased manner to public information announcements such as newspaper articles, corporate forecasts, and annual reports.

Semistrong-form market efficiency is particularly relevant to the accounting profession because accounting information is generally publicly available and provides a primary data source for security analysis. If stock markets are efficient in the semistrong form, then no amount of security analysis can consistently achieve above-normal returns. This hypothesis is disconcerting given the large number of people involved in producing, interpreting, and analyzing accounting information. Indeed, it may be the competitive effect of all these individuals attempting to profit from processing information that causes markets to be efficient. In this regard, Lorie and Hamilton [1973, p. 98] make an interesting point:

> There is a curious paradox. In order for the (efficient market) hypothesis to be true, it is necessary for many investors to disbelieve it. That is, market prices will promptly and fully reflect what is knowable about the companies whose shares are traded only if investors seek to earn superior returns, make conscientious and competent efforts to learn about the companies whose securities are traded, and analyze relevant information promptly and perceptively. If that effort were abandoned, the efficiency of the market would diminish rapidly.

Testing of semistrong-form market efficiency is commonly performed by examining stock returns following certain kinds of public information announcements. If investors can consistently obtain above-normal returns by trading at the time of a public announcement, then the stock market would be inefficient with respect to that information. For example, if above-normal returns can be made by buying stocks following announcements of increases in dividends, the stock market would not be semistrong efficient with respect to dividend announcements.

1.2.3 Strong-Form Market Efficiency

The strong form of market efficiency is the most comprehensive case. Under this hypothesis both public and private information are quickly impounded in the security price. Holders of private information, including managers and their associates, would not be able to make consistently above-normal returns using their private information. Although this extreme form of market efficiency is more difficult to accept, even for adamant believers of market efficiency, there are mechanisms that could lead to strong-form market efficiency.

Competition among the privately informed investors might be sufficient to produce prices that reflect private information. Also, other information sources could be used as a substitute for private information. Further, there may be characteristics of securities markets that cause private information rapidly to become public. One example would be uninformed investors using the stock price as an information source. If uninformed investors observe rising prices, they may infer that this is caused by good news available to privately informed investors. These mechanisms, which can lead to market efficiency, are discussed further in Chapter 2.

Testing strong-form market efficiency is difficult because the existence of private information in the market cannot be directly observed. The most common tests of strong-form market efficiency have involved the examination of the profitability of a trading strategy using the *Official Summary of Insider Trading*, which is released monthly by the SEC. This document is a record of transactions in a security made by the officers, directors, and major stockholders of that firm. If these insiders are able to make above-normal returns, the market is not strong-form efficient.

1.3 REASONS FOR MARKET INEFFICIENCY

There are several reasons why stock markets may be inefficient. Even a casual look at the statistics on the number of copies of annual reports distributed by various corporations and the hours expended by internal accountants, independent public accountants, security analysts, and investors in preparing and analyzing these reports would lead us to conclude that published statements play an important role in the dissemination of corporate information. Furthermore, several survey studies report that investors and analysts find the annual report to be the most useful information source about a company. However, many observers believe that although the market pays attention to these financial statements, investors respond in a naïve fashion to the information contained in them. This view is based on the presumption that the market is composed of a great number of individual investors, most of whom are relatively unsophisticated with limited ability to understand and interpret financial statements. These *naïve investors*, it is argued, are unable to detect subtleties in accounting reporting procedures. Thus, they often make incorrect decisions based on perceived situations that are illusory rather than substantive. Based on this view of individual investor behavior, it is argued that the market collectively reflects this inability of investors to process information. The result is that many securities are inappropriately priced.

The mispricing of securities is a central theme, for example, in the work of one of the accounting profession's most outspoken critics, Professor Abraham Briloff of The City University of New York. In his book, Briloff [1972] describes a number of cases that appear to show that the market was fooled by the accounting reports of publicly owned companies in that their stock prices were incorrectly set for some period of time.

1.4 TESTING THE EFFICIENT MARKET HYPOTHESIS

Testing the EMH has proven to be more difficult than was originally expected. Whether prices "fully reflect" information cannot be directly observed. The primary method of testing the EMH has been based on the fair-game description provided by Fama [1970]. In a "fair game," investors are not able to use their information to obtain, on average, higher than normal returns. This interpretation led to the testing of different trading strategies based on various information items. If a higher than normal return is obtained by a trading strategy using a particular information item, then the EMH is rejected with respect to that information item.

There are several experimental design problems in testing the EMH. As in the case with all hypothesis tests, testing can only reject or fail to reject the EMH at some level of confidence. The existence of efficient markets cannot be proved. Each additional test that fails to reject the EMH, however, provides further evidence that the EMH is a reasonable description of how securities markets operate.

The ability to reject a hypothesis depends both on the power of the test and on the number of independent times the test is performed. If the test is too weak, then the EMH is more difficult to reject. On the other hand, rejection of the EMH in one test is not sufficient to reject it in general. Because stock returns are subject to uncertainty, above-normal returns for a given trading strategy will occur sometimes if a sufficient number of tests is made. As more and more tests are performed, rejections of the EMH will randomly occur with a probability equal to the confidence level used for the tests even though the market is efficient.

Assurance that the market is inefficient with respect to a specific information item can be obtained by examining stock returns over different time periods. If above-normal returns can be earned using a specific type of information item in many different years, then it is reasonable to conclude that the market is reacting inefficiently to that type of information.

A major problem in testing the EMH is determining what constitutes "normal" or "expected" returns. Since the EMH is usually tested by examining deviations from expected returns, it is necessary to estimate expected returns. The most common approach used to estimate expected returns is the capital asset pricing model (CAPM) and its derivatives. Other models derived from *arbitrage pricing theory* have recently been proposed. A lack of general agreement on the proper model of expected returns has implications for testing the EMH. If a test of an investment strategy yields returns that are different than expected, the results may be due to a misspecification of the *expected returns model*. An alternative approach used in recent literature and suggested in Chapter 5 of this book is to assume that the market is efficient and that returns are appropriate. Then empirical work can be used to make inferences about the appropriateness of alternative pricing models.

1.4.1 The Capital Asset Pricing Model

The CAPM is the generally accepted model for determining expected returns. This model, developed by Sharpe [1964], Lintner [1965], and Mossin [1966], is based on individual investors holding diversified portfolios to obtain the maximum return for a given level of risk. The model is derived from the following assumptions:

1. Investors have the same investment horizons and the same beliefs about the distribution of each security's future returns.
2. Beliefs about the distribution of future returns are normally distributed or investors' preferences are based only on the mean and variance of the distribution.
3. Investors are risk averse (this may be characterized as a preference for a smaller variance of returns for a given expected return).
4. Investors are able to borrow or lend an unlimited amount of a riskless security (a security with a zero variance return).
5. There are no transaction costs for investors.

With multiple securities, investors are concerned with expectations about portfolio returns. Moreover, all individual securities are evaluated with respect to their relationship to the total portfolio. Thus the risk of an individual security is its contribution to the overall portfolio risk, which is usually a value quite different from a measure of the individual security's risk as reflected by the variability of its return.

Figure 1-1 depicts graphically the investment opportunities facing an investor in terms of the expected return and risk of a portfolio. The shaded region represents all possible combinations of risky securities. If an investor were forced to choose from this set of portfolios, only those on the upper left-hand boundary of the shaded region would be selected since these dominate other portfolios. That is, these are the portfolios that provide the highest return for a given level of risk or, alternatively, the lowest risk for a given rate of return. (These portfolios are described as *mean-variance efficient*, when risk is measured by the portfolios' variance, which is different from market efficiency.) The exact portfolio selected would depend on the investor's preferences, tastes, and financial situation.

When the assumption is added that all investors can borrow or lend at some riskless rate, L, which is determined exogenously, the opportunities available are increased. Now an investor can borrow (or lend) at the rate L, the rate at which there is zero risk, say, a government bond, and combine this amount with an investment in portfolio M to attain any combination on the line LMN. (The investor could do the same with portfolio P; however, all portfolios on line

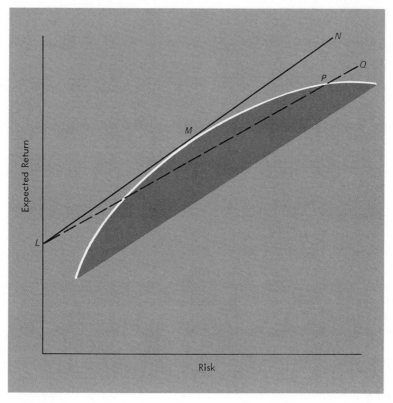

FIGURE 1-1

LPQ are inferior to portfolios on *LMN* in that for every level of risk a higher return is attainable on line *LMN* than on line *LPQ*). By investing part of the available funds at rate *L* and the remainder in portfolio *M*, an investor can achieve any point on the line segment *LM*, depending on the percentage invested in each component. Similarly, by borrowing at rate *L* and using these borrowed funds to increase the investment in portfolio *M*, an investor can attain any point on line segment *MN*. This borrowing procedure is called purchasing securities on margin. Each investor, depending on personal preferences, tastes, and financial situation, invests the appropriate amount of funds in portfolio *M* and borrows or lends the appropriate amount at rate *L* to attain the desired risk-return combination. An investor desiring a relatively low-risk position splits the total invested funds between the riskless asset *L* and the risky portfolio *M*. An investor willing to take on more risk to obtain a higher return borrows at the risk-free rate and invests all available funds in the risky portfolio *M*.

If Figure 1-1 is viewed as the set of investment opportunities available for a specific individual, any attempt to aggregate these opportunities across all investors faces the problem that individual investors hold different beliefs about the composition of portfolio *M*. That is, if investors possess differing amounts of information and abilities to process this information, then their expectations about the levels of risk and return will also differ. This problem is eliminated if the assumption is made that all investors hold identical beliefs about the probability distributions of the values of each security at the end of some identical investment horizon. Under this assumption, everyone reaches the same conclusion about the composition of portfolio *M*, which can then be viewed as representing the market.

Portfolio *M* comprises all the shares outstanding of all the securities in the market. Furthermore, so that all securities can be held, the prices of those securities must adjust until portfolio *M* contains each security in proportion to its total market value. This portfolio is called the *market portfolio*, and the line *LMN*, which represents the dominant investment opportunities, is called the *capital market line*. Thus the relationship between risk and return for any portfolio on the capital market line is linear. An expected return in excess of the riskless rate *L* is given by the amount of risk borne by the portfolio, multiplied by the slope of the capital market line, which is called the *market price of risk*. (Mathematically the "rise" in a straight line is given by the product of "run" multiplied by the line's slope.)

The most frequently used measure of total risk for a security or portfolio is its variance. However, this is not the risk measure that determines the expected excess return, called the risk premium. When combining securities into a portfolio, the expected portfolio return is equal to a weighted average of the expected individual security returns. The weights are the fractions of the total dollar value of the portfolio represented by each security. However, the variance of the portfolio return is not necessarily (or usually) the weighted average of the variances of the individual security returns. The variance of the portfolio return is affected by the degree to which the expected security returns move together, that is, by their covariability. Thus if when one security return rises, a second falls, and vice versa, then investing equally in both reduces the variability of the resulting portfolio. This covariability is measured by the covariance of the individual security's returns with the market portfolio. For example, if the return on an investment does not vary regardless of changes in the return on the market portfolio, its covariability is zero, whereas if its return moves exactly with the market, its covariability is one. (See Appendix A for a discussion of variance and covariance.)

When combining securities into a portfolio, the covariance of the portfolio with the market portfolio is a weighted average of the covariances of the security returns in the portfolio with the market portfolio. By increasing the number of securities in the portfolio, an investor is able to eliminate virtually all of the variability of the portfolio's expected returns except that portion that is due to the covariance of the portfolio returns with the return on the market portfolio. This covariance is the portfolio's systematic risk, and is that part of the portfolio's total risk for which an investor can expect to be rewarded by receiving a risk premium.

The crucial aspect in the CAPM is that each security has an expected return that is related to its risk. This risk is measured by the security's systematic movements with the overall market. Furthermore, this systematic risk cannot be eliminated by merely increasing the number of securities in an investor's portfolio. On the other hand, no part of the expected return for a security is provided by that variability or price movement that is not in concert with the market since it can be eliminated by increasing portfolio diversification. The expected return on a security is solely a function of the covariability of the individual security's return with the market's return.

The *beta* of a security or portfolio is defined as the systematic risk of that security or portfolio expressed in units of market risk. The beta of the market portfolio is 1.0 since the covariance of a portfolio with itself is just its variance. Securities or portfolios with betas of less than 1.0 have less systematic risk than the overall market, and those with betas greater than 1.0 have more. If the expected excess return on the market portfolio during a period is 10 percent, a security with a beta of 2.0 would be expected to yield, on the average, an excess return of 20 percent. Similarly, for an expected market decline of 10 percent, the same security can be expected to lose 20 percent on the average. When observing actual returns, there are differences between the observed security returns and the component explained by the market. This difference is due to the security's nonsystematic risk, the risk avoidable through diversification.

The CAPM offers a simple formula that yields the expected returns for individual securities. This formula is described in more detail in Appendix B. The simplicity of the formula, however, is created by the stringency of the assumptions underlying the CAPM. Efforts to relax these assumptions result in more complex derivatives of the CAPM, which are described in Chapter 5.

Although the CAPM has received considerable attention, the expectational nature of the model creates problems in performing empirical tests. Expectations are not directly observable. An alternative approach is to suggest that returns can be described by the market model (also described in Appendix B). The market model states that returns are a linear function of the return on the market. Return variance explained by the market would be systematic, whereas the remaining variance represents unsystematic risk. Any return not explained by the market is considered an abnormal return.

Applying the market model to tests of market efficiency involves the examination of abnormal returns from a trading strategy. A trading strategy that consistently generates abnormal returns would suggest rejecting market efficiency. But an alternative explanation is that the pricing model (in this case, the market model) is misspecified. If the appropriate pricing model were used, no abnormal returns would have been found. This dilemma illustrates the joint hypothesis nature of tests of market efficiency. A rejection of market efficiency can generally be attributed to an inappropriate pricing model based on the absence of arbitrage opportunities is sug-empirical tests provide more information about the appropriate pricing model. A further discussion of this approach is given in Chapter 5.

1.4.2 Arbitrage Pricing Models

In recent years, other pricing models have been proposed. A pricing model based on the absence of arbitrage opportunities is suggested by Ross [1976, 1977]. Arbitrage pricing theory is based on the argument that securities with identical returns should be priced the same. If securities with identical returns were priced differently, then an individual could buy one and sell the other to obtain a sure profit with no investment. Arbitrage pricing theory is applied by combining existing assets to duplicate the returns of the asset of interest. Black and Scholes [1973] are able to combine shares of stock and a riskless asset to price options. But, in general, it is difficult to construct these combinations to establish an identical return series for most investments.

Ross [1976, 1977] determines that a multifactor model can be used to approximate the return series of every security if there are no arbitrage opportunities. There are several advantages to this approach over the capital asset pricing model. First, the stringent assumptions about the return distributions and individual preferences are no longer necessary. Second, knowledge of the market return is not necessary. (See Appendix B.3 for a further discussion.)

There are several problems, however, with the arbitrage pricing model. The factors comprising the model are not identified in the process of developing the model. Even the number of factors in unknown. The factors are imbedded in the return structure of securities.

These factors can, perhaps, be elicited and identified through factor analysis on past data; but a pricing model is based on expectational data that are not directly observable.

Jarrow [1983] points out that the arbitrage pricing model is fundamentally different from the capital asset pricing model. The arbitrage pricing model is based on the relationship between prices and cannot be used to determine all prices endogenously. Some prices have to be specified exogenously to provide a basis for comparison. The capital asset pricing model, on the other hand, is based directly on expectations, and all prices are determined endogenously.

Little empirical work has been done with the arbitrage pricing model. Attempts to test the arbitrage pricing model are described in Section 5.3. The arbitrage pricing model has also been used to attempt to explain divergencies from market efficiency discovered using of the capital asset pricing model. The relevant papers are discussed in the sections related to the specific information event of interest.

1.5 SUMMARY

The discussion to this point has centered on the relationship between information and the market for corporate securities. The efficient market hypothesis states that information is quickly impounded by the market and fully reflected in the prices. Weak, semi-strong, and strong forms of market efficiency may be defined based on the availability of the information. Empirical tests of these hypotheses, however, are fraught with difficulties. The most difficult problem is choosing an expected returns model that permits the researcher to measure expected returns correctly. A misspecification of the expected returns model can lead to an inappropriate conclusion about the efficiency of markets.

In Chapter 2, the theory of efficient markets is reviewed. Although Fama [1970] defined efficient markets as having prices that fully reflect information, recent research indicates that there is disagreement on exactly what "fully reflect" means. Various definitions of market efficiency are discussed as are the dynamic processes that lead to market efficiency.

Chapters 3 and 4 review the evidence from tests of efficient markets. These chapters are organized by the type of information used in the test. In Chapter 3, studies of market efficiency using nonaccounting information are examined. Chapter 4 considers tests of market efficiency based on accounting information.

In Chapter 5 the pricing models are reexamined based on the empirical evidence in the prior two chapters. The effects of relaxing the assumptions of the CAPM are discussed and related to the empirical results.

The final chapter reviews the implications of market efficiency for accounting. The reader who wishes to skip the details of the empirical research may wish to turn immediately to Chapter 6. Chapter 6 is self-contained.

CHAPTER TWO

The Theory
of Efficient Markets

In Chapter 1 the *efficient market hypothesis* (EMH) is characterized by the existence of a set of prices that fully reflect information. The exact meaning of "fully reflect," however, is unclear and is the focus of recent debate. Information is reflected by security prices when prices change because of changes in investor beliefs. The new beliefs affect prices through changes in demand. The process of disseminating and analyzing information to develop new expectations about future prices determines the degree of efficiency in the market.

One approach to characterizing market efficiency is to ignore dissemination issues and assume that investors have common expectations. This approach is concerned with the accuracy of these price expectations. There are several problems with this approach. If investor expectations diverge, whose expectations should be used to test market efficiency? And even if everyone has the same expectations, how can those expectations be observed? Finally, what benchmark should be used to test the accuracy of those expectations? These problems lead to alternative approaches to characterizing market efficiency.

Another approach to characterizing market efficiency is to assume that prices "fully reflect" the information available to all investors. Prices with full dissemination of information are used as benchmarks for determining market efficiency. The question that is addressed through this approach is whether prices with partial dissemination of information are equal to prices with full dissemination of information. This approach also has testing problems. How can the researcher know when all investors have the information such that existing prices can be used as a test benchmark? And if this complete dissemination of information takes place at a date later than the test period, how much of the benchmark price reflects "normal" returns over that time period?

These definitions of an efficient market are static. They are not accompanied by a dynamic process that produces the set of efficient prices. Several theories for achieving an efficient market have been suggested. These theories begin by assuming an asymmetric distribution of information and proceed to describe how prices would adjust to reflect this information. One theory asserts that privately informed investors engage in speculation based on their information. The demand due to speculation by privately informed investors causes changes in prices to reflect the private information. Another theory, called the *rational expectations theory*, allows investors without private information to infer that information from prices. If privately informed investors receive good news about a particular security, they increase their demand, which in turn increases prices. Uninformed investors observe the increase in prices and infer that the privately informed investors have received good news. Prices then adjust as if every investor has the information.

These theories and definitions are not testable unless they have some empirical content. If a theory or definition describes a relationship between unobservable phenomena, then that theory or definition provides little benefit to the scientist who must verify the theory's predictions with observable variables. Theories and definitions with empirical content are useful in interpreting the research results reviewed in the following chapters.

2.1 USING ACCURACY OF PRICE EXPECTATIONS TO DEFINE MARKET EFFICIENCY

The idea of market efficiency has its origins in the notion of intrinsic value. Although the value of most goods has been accepted to be a function of consumer beliefs, preferences, and endowments, securities have often been treated as having a value independent of these consumer characteristics. Instead, intrinsic value is based uniquely on the characteristics of the firm that issues the security.

If the security price differs from the intrinsic value, then the security is considered overpriced or underpriced. The price of a security, however, depends not only on the characteristics of the firm, but also on the demand for the security. The value for a security, as with any other good, depends on the consumer (investor).

Fama [1970] described an efficient market as having prices that "fully reflect" available information. He recognized, however, that a more formal definition is necessary to obtain empirical implications. Hence, in the same paper, Fama attempted to formalize this definition. He stated that a market is efficient with respect to an information set if the expected future price conditioned on that information is equal, on average, to the actual future price. The implication of this definition is that there exists a distribution of future prices and that market efficiency occurs when the expected price conditioned on a set of information is equal to the expected value of this distribution of future prices.

This definition suffers from several operational difficulties. First, expected prices are unobservable. Second, the definition is silent on just whose expectations are involved. Finally, LeRoy [1976] shows that Fama's set of equations defining market efficiency are tautological in that the expected difference between expected and actual values of a stochastic process is zero.

Fama [1976] attempts to clarify his formalization of the definition of market efficiency by explicitly defining a density function of future prices conditioned on the set of information available in the present period. This density function of future prices is then compared with the density function of future prices obtained conditional upon the information actually used by the market. Any differences in the density functions is treated as a sign of market inefficiency. Fama recognizes that this definition is too general to have testable implications and suggests the need for an equilibrium model to establish the relationship between the present price and the density function of future prices conditioned on the information used by the market. With this addition, empirical tests become joint tests of this equilibrium model and market efficiency.

Using future price distributions to define market efficiency illustrates the importance of having an equilibrium return model for testing market efficiency. A return model is necessary to establish the link between expected returns (prices) and actual returns (prices). Without an acceptable equilibrium return model, the EMH cannot be tested.

Relating price expectations with future price distributions is also the basis for a branch of economic literature known as *rational expectations*. A rational expectations equilibrium occurs when expectations are realized in a future period. Realizations of future events, including prices, have a direct link with present prices. For example, present prices influence production decisions that, in turn, affect future prices. Present prices also act as aggregators of diverse beliefs caused by investors having different information. A fully revealing rational expectations equilibrium occurs when prices reveal all the private information held by individual investors. This revelation occurs because investors use their private information to demand securities, which then affects the prices of those securities. A more complete discussion of rational expectations is found in Grossman [1981].

2.2 DEFINING MARKET EFFICIENCY BASED ON INFORMATION DISTRIBUTION

The previous section provided definitions of market efficiency using expectations conditioned on some information set. The question of whose expectations should be used was not resolved. With *homogeneous beliefs*, the choice of whose expectations to use is simplified. Rubinstein [1975, p. 812] states:

> In a perfect and competitive economy composed of rational individuals with homogeneous beliefs about future prices, by any meaningful definition present security prices must fully reflect all available information about future prices.

The problem in defining market efficiency occurs when investors have *heterogeneous beliefs*. Not only do heterogeneous beliefs make it difficult to define market efficiency, but they also lead to a situation in which some investors perceive prices as not "fully reflecting" their information.

Beaver [1981] offers a definition of market efficiency based on the information distribution. Specifically, a market is defined as efficient with respect to a specific information set if the price that exists is the same as the price that would exist if everyone has that information set.

Basing a definition of market efficiency on prices that would exist if everyone has the information is appealing for two reasons. First, with this definition market efficiency can exist in a world with heterogeneous beliefs. Individual investors would not need to perceive the market as efficient for efficiency to exist.

Second, market efficiency can be defined with respect to separate information sets. Beaver carries this definition farther by defining market efficiency with respect to individual signals as well as with respect to the information system generating those signals.

An interesting implication of this definition is that the market is efficient by definition with respect to information that is distributed to everyone. This definition would seem to indicate that weak and semistrong forms of market inefficiency could not exist. But Beaver argues that even if the information is publicly available, there may still exist costs of obtaining the information to some investors. For example, a public announcement of earnings may be made by a company official, but there is a time delay before this information is published in *The Wall Street Journal*. Further, some investors may not even have easy access to *The Wall Street Journal*. Therefore, apparent public disclosures may only be partially disseminated, and market inefficiences under Beaver's definition could result. This situation is especially true for the short time following the initial announcement.

Beaver points out that his definition can also allow for problems in processing information. If information processing is conceptualized as moving from "raw" information to "refined" information, then a market is efficient if the price is the same as the price would be if everyone had the refined information.

Even though Beaver's definition allows the empiricist to specify the information system being studied, there are still problems in testing this definition of market efficiency. To test this form of market efficiency, the researcher must be able to determine when all investors have the information and then use that price as the benchmark. But it is typically difficult to observe when everyone has the information. If it is assumed that everyone has the information at a later date, then the researcher must compare prices over two dates. These prices should differ because of "normal" returns over that time period. Therefore, any test of market efficiency under Beaver's definition still requires the use of a pricing model to determine "normal" returns. The empirical implications of these various definitions of market efficiency are discussed further in Section 2.4.

Defining market efficiency has caused considerable confusion because of existing definitions of efficiency in the economics literature. *Pareto efficiency* occurs in markets when no further reallocations of goods can improve the welfare of some without harming others. Easley and Jarrow [1982] modify the definition of Pareto economic efficiency to define market efficiency in terms of allocations of securities rather than in terms of prices. Easley and Jarrow define a market as efficient with respect to an information distribution if investors receive allocations that cannot be improved through the use of their respective information. Although this definition of market efficiency is more consistent with economic definitions of efficiency, the problem of testing for market efficiency is not resolved. In fact, Jarrow and Easley claim that the capital asset pricing model cannot be used to test for market efficiency because the model is derived from the assumption that all investors already have equal access to information.

2.3 DYNAMIC PROCESSES LEADING TO MARKET EFFICIENCY

The previous sections of this chapter contain several definitions of market efficiency. Each definition is characterized by a static environment in which market efficiency would exist. The definitions, however, are silent on the dynamic process that leads to that equilibrium. This section reviews several theories of the dynamic process for achieving market efficiency.

Figlewski [1978] attempts to explain how market efficiency is achieved when investors have *different information*. He defines an efficient market as a market with a price that appropriately weighs the quality of the information held by each investor. But the weight of an investor's beliefs in determining the market price is a function of the investor's wealth. Wealthier investors normally have a greater influence on the market price. The issue is whether an investor's wealth adjusts such that the influence of that investor on the price precisely reflects the quality of that investor's information. Figlewski finds that in the short run the direction of the change in wealth is such that the market efficiently weighs the quality of the information.

Beaver [1981] defines efficient markets in terms of the configuration of information held by investors. Prices that occur when everyone has the information are efficient by definition and are referred to as *full-information prices*. Attaining market efficiency under this definition is only a problem if there is an asymmetric distribution of information. Full-information prices occur automatically if there is some market mechanism to distribute the information uniformly. Full-information prices may also occur through the speculative behavior of privately informed investors.

There are several mechanisms in stock markets that would cause a rapid dissemination of privately held information. As mentioned in Chapter 1, the SEC enforces disclosure requirements. Also, information has characteristics that make it difficult to keep it private. These characteristics include the fact that information can be used without being consumed and it is difficult to exclude nonpurchasers. Exclusion of nonpurchasers is difficult because once an investor uses information, that investor would be willing to sell it. The price of information would be driven quickly to zero as other informed investors attempt to sell the same information. The zero price occurs because of competition and the lack of value of the information to the seller once the information has been used. Therefore, the market for information leads to its rapid dissemination. Upon using the information to take a speculative position, the seller may even be willing to pay for the dissemination of the information to ensure that prices adjust to reflect it.

Speculative behavior on the part of privately informed investors can also lead directly to full-information prices. If private information is about to be publicly released and privately informed investors know the full-information price, then these investors have incentives to trade on their private information until the full-information price is reached. In this manner, efficient prices can be attained without a complete distribution of the information. There are several conditions that may restrict the actions of the privately informed investors such that the market would not achieve efficiency. Restrictions on borrowing and short sales or the presence of other transaction costs may inhibit privately informed investors from trading to the extent necessary to make prices efficient.

Still another way that uninformed investors could obtain private information is through observing prices. Prices are affected by the demand of privately informed investors and, therefore, are influenced by private information. Kihlstrom and Mirman [1975] and Radner [1979] have examined conditions under which prices completely reveal information, and Grossman [1976] has provided an example of completely revealing prices. Using prices to infer information is a form of rational expectations. If prices are completely revealing, then all investors become informed and the market is efficient by Beaver's definition.

There are, however, several problems with a fully revealing rational-expectations equilibrium. The cognitive capabilities of the investors need to be enormous to be able to infer information from prices. Also, a fully revealing rational-expectations equilibrium may not exist with costly information. Investors have no incentives to purchase costly information if it is immediately revealed in prices. No speculative positions would be taken. Grossman and Stiglitz [1980] suggest that the stock market must be slightly inefficient to allow purchasers of information to obtain a reasonable return.

This section has reviewed dynamic processes that can lead to efficient markets. There are no empirical tests attempting to identify the actual process the market uses to incorporate information, but the existence of relatively efficient markets, no matter how defined, appears plausible given the variety of processes that can lead to efficient prices.

2.4 IMPLICATIONS FOR EMPIRICAL RESEARCH

Most of the papers defining market efficiency have followed rather than preceded attempts to test market efficiency. This approach is partially due to questions raised about early empirical research on market efficiency. Did the specific empirical research test for market efficiency? What assumptions are necessary for a valid test of market efficiency? Can a valid test for market efficiency be operationalized? These questions and others led to a reevaluation of the "fully reflect" definition of market efficiency. Whether these new definitions provide any insights on how to test for market efficiency is the topic of this section.

Definitions of market efficiency relate to accurate expectations and, hence, require models to represent expected returns. These expected returns act as a link between present prices and future prices. The market is efficient if the present prices plus expected returns have a distribution that coincides with the distribution of future prices. The reliance of a test of market efficiency on an expected returns model makes any test of market efficiency a joint test of the expected returns model and market efficiency. Any observed deviation from market efficiency in empirical tests may be due to an inappropriate expected returns model.

The problems of testing market efficiency defined as the prices that would exist if everyone had the information are somewhat similar to those encountered when expectations are embodied in the definition. Prices are efficient, by definition, when everyone has the information, so the focus is on situations when information is not available to all investors. The comparison is made between present prices with a partial distribution of the information and future prices with a complete distribution of the information. Any difference in the two prices that could not be explained by expected returns is a sign of market inefficiency. Therefore, an expected returns model is still necessary as well as knowledge of when the information is completely distributed.

The problem of specifying an appropriate expected returns model can be partially overcome by examining returns over a very short time period. Any equilibrium pricing model yields zero expected returns as the time period approaches zero. If a nonzero expected return existed over an instantaneous time period, then the original price is not in equilibrium. Any returns that deviate substantially from zero in the short run are due primarily to factors beyond an expected returns model. Therefore, tests of market efficiency examining short-run price adjustments subsequent to information releases are more reliable than are analyses of long-term returns, which are more susceptible to the use of an inappropriate expected returns model.

The empirical implications of the definitions of market efficiency are essentially the same. The general approach is to attempt to discern abnormal returns following information events. All the definitions rely on the choice of an appropriate pricing model. Interpretations of the empirical results may differ with the definition, however. Beaver's definition assumes that the market is efficient with respect to public information (if it is completely disseminated). Therefore, any observance of an abnormal return following a public information event can be solely attributed to a misspecified pricing model rather than to a rejection of either the pricing model or market efficiency.

Chapters 3 and 4 review a number of studies that examine returns following public information events in spite of Beaver's definition of market efficiency. Chapter 5 reevaluates these studies on the assumption that they are really tests of pricing models. Findings of abnormal returns indicate that a misspecified pricing model is being used and, also, give us information about the characteristics of the correct pricing model. Redirecting the focus of research from tests of market efficiency to tests of pricing models is one of the major purposes of this book.

2.5 SUMMARY

This chapter identifies two basic approaches to defining market efficiency: one relates existing prices to expectations of future prices; the other assumes that the market is efficient with respect to some information if the price is the same as the price in a market in which everyone has the information.

Theories that describe how the market achieves efficiency are also discussed. Of primary interest is how information is disseminated among the participants in the market and how the participants act on the information. Privately informed investors attempt to obtain a profit on their information through speculation and sale, while uninformed investors attempt to avoid losses by purchasing the information or using the security's price as an information source. This chapter examines how these actions can lead to efficient prices.

Empirical tests of market efficiency, no matter which definition is used, require a model of expected returns. Tests of market efficiency, then, become joint tests of the pricing model and market efficiency. If the information is public, however, then Beaver's definition of market efficiency suggests that a test of returns following the information release is only a test of the pricing model because the market is assumed to be efficient with respect to public information.

CHAPTER THREE

Tests of Market Efficiency Using Nonaccounting Information

This chapter reviews tests of the EMH using nonaccounting information. The reasons for including a chapter on nonaccounting evidence are (1) to provide results that are comparable to those using accounting variables, which are reviewed in Chapter 4, and (2) to provide a basis for discussing alternative pricing models in Chapter 5.

The initial sections of this chapter are based on the weak, semi-strong, and strong forms of market efficiency. Empirical tests of each of these forms are reviewed and discussed. These tests examine primarily the profitability of trading on certain types of information.

The latter sections are devoted to several topics not easily synthesized into the framework of the initial sections. For example, a recent approach to testing market efficiency involves the examination of price variances. Studies using this approach attempt to determine if price variability in the short run is inconsistent given the variability of long-run returns. Higher than normal variance in the short run, it is hypothesized, could be caused by an overreaction to information.

Market efficiency is also closely tied to the concept of arbitrage. An arbitrage opportunity allows an investor, without risk of loss, to make a positive return with a zero investment. An arbitrage opportunity, therefore, constitutes a violation of market efficiency. Several studies that imply the existence of arbitrage opportunities are discussed.

Takeover bids, which offer premiums above the existing stock price, also have implications for market efficiency. If a market is efficient with respect to all forms of information (including strong-form efficiency), then a firm should not be willing to pay more than the market share price to acquire control of another firm.

Also, issues of market efficiency have been studied in laboratory settings. Experimental markets are established with a controlled flow of information. Prices are then determined by having participants transact among themselves. This approach can provide insights on how investors use information and how information becomes impounded in prices in actual security markets.

In Chapter 2 different definitions of market efficiency are offered. One definition stated that private information is a necessary but not sufficient condition for market inefficiency to occur. In other words, markets impound public information in prices. Therefore, there would be no tests of weak-form or semistrong-form market information. Since this definition is not universally accepted, only studies of returns following public information events (which include past prices as a source of information) are reviewed. In these studies, any evidence of abnormal returns following information events is an indication of either an inefficient market or a misspecified pricing model. Chapter 5 reexamines these findings by assuming that the market is efficient and attempts to make inferences about the pricing model.

3.1 TESTS OF WEAK-FORM MARKET EFFICIENCY

As described in Chapter 1, the weak form of the EMH states that an investor cannot use past security price information to earn a portfolio return consistently in excess of the return that is commensurate with the portfolio's risk. Another way to state this hypothesis is that the investor who uses past security price data to choose a portfolio will not consistently outperform an investor who buys and holds a random portfolio of the same risk. Under weak-form efficiency, technical analysis (charting of prices, etc.) alone will not yield superior portfolio performance.

Much of the early research on the weak form of the EMH centered on the question of whether security prices follow a random walk. These studies, which were reviewed in Chapter 1, are not able to reject the null hypothesis that security prices follow a random walk. The conclusion suggested by the authors is that the best estimate of future prices is the present price. Past prices provide no information about future prices if prices follow a random walk.

Samuelson [1965] attempts to relate the random walk of prices with an efficient use of information by proving that properly anticipated prices fluctuate randomly. LeRoy [1973], however, pointed out that Samuelson's proof depends on an exogenously given expected rate of return. If returns are determined within an equilibrium framework, expected returns depend on both the riskiness of the stock and the risk aversion of investors. If so, expected returns will not necessarily be independent over time. Prices may not follow a random walk and yet they still may be efficient. Therefore, the early tests of market efficiency are not sufficiently well-specified to resolve the question.

Although the past time series of prices by itself tells us nothing about market efficiency, components of those prices are still useful in testing for market efficiency. In particular, risk-adjusted (or abnormal) returns should not be correlated and, hence, they should be independent over time. If a significant correlation of abnormal returns over time exists for a security, then investors could use this information in trading to secure abnormal returns and the market would be inefficient. To test this idea empirically requires a pricing model to determine the expected abnormal return. Thus, any test of weak-form market efficiency becomes a joint test of both the pricing model and market efficiency.

There have been three major approaches used to test for the dependence of returns over time: *serial correlation tests*, *filter rule tests*, and *cyclical tests*. All three of these tests are related, with the serial correlation tests being the most general.

3.1.1 Serial Correlation Tests

Serial correlation measures the association between two elements in a time series separated by a constant number of time periods. The number of time periods that separate the two elements is known as the order of the serial correlation. For example, first-order serial correlation examines the association of elements one time period apart.

Tests performed by Schwartz and Whitcomb [1977a, 1977b] and Rosenberg and Rudd [1982] indicate that the first-order serial correlation of daily return residuals from the market model are small but significantly negative. This implies that return residuals of one sign tend to be followed by return residuals of the opposite sign using daily data. These results are not consistent with market efficiency. However, no trading strategies have been tested to determine if an abnormal return can be made after allowing for transaction costs.

There are several alternative explanations for the negative first-order serial correlation in daily residuals. Market makers and the existence of discrete rather than continuous prices may cause residuals to have negative serial correlation. Both these phenomena cause more reversals in residual series even though equilibrium residuals are independent. In addition, daily returns may be measured with error because they are calculated from the price of the last trade of the day. The last trade of the day may have taken place hours before closing. Combining this phenomenon with a market index comprised of securities that trade near closing could cause a negative first-order serial correlation for return residuals. These are characteristics of the stock market and do not allow traders to make abnormal returns.

3.1.2 Filter Rule Tests

An alternative method of testing weak-form market efficiency is by examining filter rules. Employing a filter rule, if a stock's price advances by a certain percentage over a previous low point, it is bought. If the stock declines from a previous high point, it is sold when the decline exceeds a specified percentage. Alexander [1961] finds that his filter rules produced very large rates of return, particularly for small filters (for example, 5 percent). However, when transactions costs are considered, the abnormal returns disappear for all filter rules. Further research into the use of filter rules by Fama [1965] and Fama and Blume [1966] fails to show an abnormal rate of return for the filter rules studied.

Another filter rule procedure is proposed by Levy [1967]. Using a relative strength method based on the ratio of a stock's current price to its average price, he finds a rule that yielded an abnormal portfolio return. However, Jensen [1967] points out that Levy tests his technical model on the same data that are used to select the model. Such a validation procedure biases the results in favor of the model and is inappropriate statistically. When Jensen and Bennington [1970] test Levy's procedure on other sets of data, no significant abnormal return is found.

Beaver and Landsman [1981] test a longer-range filter rule. They divide securities into winners and losers based on their performance in the previous 20 months. They then examine the abnormal returns of the two portfolios in the subsequent months. No significant differences exist between the two portfolios.

3.1.3 Cyclical Tests

Spectral analysis is a statistical method of testing for cyclical behavior in a time series. Granger and Morgenstern [1963] use this approach on stock prices but find no significant relationships. Recently, tests have been performed on returns during different days of the week and months of the year. These tests have yielded some surprising results.

Cross [1973], French [1980], and Gibbons and Hess [1981] all document that raw returns on Mondays are significantly lower than the raw returns on other days of the week. Lakonishok and Levi [1982] attempt to explain this behavior through delays in settling transactions. Settlement takes place five business days after the transaction. An additional day for check clearing makes Friday an advantageous day to buy and Monday a good day to sell. Lakonishok and Levi find that this market mechanism explains the low returns on Monday for recent years but not for earlier years.

As mentioned earlier, raw returns may have nonrandom patterns and still be consistent with market efficiency. Risk-adjusted returns, however, can be used to test for market efficiency. Gibbons and Hess [1981] find no significant Monday effects when using residuals from the market model.

Bonin and Moses [1974] and Rozeff and Kinney [1976] observe that there have been seasonal patterns in stock prices. In particular, Rozeff and Kinney note that stock returns in January have been significantly higher than in other months. Once again, however, these tests are performed on raw returns. When Rozeff and Kinney use market-based pricing models to estimate return residuals, the January effect disappears.

In summary, the weak form of market efficiency cannot be tested using statistical tests on stock prices and raw returns. Even though patterns in price movements have been observed, the stock market may still be efficient. A pricing model is necessary to determine risk-adjusted returns. The resulting risk-adjusted returns should not exhibit any predictable pattern over time.

The evidence indicates that daily return residuals tend to have negative first-order serial correlation. In other words, risk-adjusted returns tend to have opposite signs from day to day. This reversal phenomenon is inconsistent with market efficiency, but there may be measurement errors and market mechanisms causing these results. Also, a successful trading rule using transaction costs has not yet been demonstrated. The evidence to date is consistent with the inability to achieve abnormal returns through the use of past prices. These results are also consistent with the market model being the appropriate pricing model if the market is assumed efficient with respect to past prices.

3.2 TESTS OF SEMISTRONG-FORM MARKET EFFICIENCY

Semistrong-form market efficiency describes a market that quickly impounds all publicly available information. The concept subsumes weak-form efficiency. In terms of a trading strategy, an investor would not be able to make abnormal returns from the use of public information in a market that is semistrong efficient. One type of public information is financial accounting reports. These reports are an important component of information available to investors and are studied separately in Chapter 4. This section's focus is on other types of available information and their relationship to market efficiency.

Tests of the semistrong form of the EMH have studied the reaction of security prices to various types of information announcements. If the market is efficient, in the semistrong sense, expectations exist concerning security price behavior surrounding a public announcement. If the announcement has some economic significance, then there should be some reaction; however, the EMH would predict this reaction to occur prior to or almost immediately upon the public announcement. Since the information may be learned by the investment community from alternative information sources prior to its public announcement, the existence of a price reaction prior to the public announcement would not be unusual. Furthermore, a reaction immediately upon the announcement date could be caused by any additional information not anticipated by or previously disclosed to the market participants. There should be no discernible price reaction following the announcement because the market participants would unbiasedly adjust market prices immediately (or nearly so), thereby removing any possibility for future abnormal returns. Sections 3.2.1 through 3.2.7 examine several information events, including stock splits, block traders, and dividend announcements.

3.2.1 Stock Splits

The first study of the semistrong form of the EMH using risk-adjusted returns was conducted by Fama, Fisher, Jensen, and Roll [1969], who considered the behavior of abnormal security returns following stock splits. Since stock splits are frequently associated with increased dividend payouts, it would be expected that split announcements would contain some economic information. Fama et al. found that there is considerable market reaction prior to stock splits. In fact, the average cumulative abnormal security return for the 30-month period up to the month of the split is in excess of 30 percent. This figure represents a return significantly above a normal rate of return from buying and holding a portfolio of similar risk.

The behavior of the security prices after the stock split is exactly what the EMH would predict. Following the split, no additional extraordinary returns are found based on the knowledge of the split. The average cumulative abnormal return, which is increasing prior to the split, ceases to increase (or decrease) significantly in the periods following the split.

A more recent study of stock splits and market efficiency is performed by Charest [1978a]. He points out that Fama et al. use the day of the stock split as the announcement date. Charest examined returns surrounding the date the stock split is proposed, the date the stock split is approved by shareholders, and the date of the actual stock split. He finds that some abnormal returns could be obtained following stock split proposals in the 1950s but that, in general, the market appears to be efficient with respect to stock splits.

3.2.2 Block Trades

With market efficiency, prices should reflect information about the value of a security. But prices are a function of the supply and demand for securities, and temporary imbalances may occur if a large supply of securities is suddenly placed on the market. Recent studies have examined whether block trades (usually defined to be greater than 10,000 to 50,000 shares) have an effect on prices.

Scholes [1972] looks at daily returns surrounding the sale of a block of shares. He observes a significant drop in prices. Scholes attributes this permanent drop in prices to an information effect. The act of selling a large number of shares is perceived by the market as a reflection of negative information held by the seller. If the price drop is caused by selling pressure, then the price should rebound to its prior level once the market assimilates the shares.

Kraus and Stoll [1972] and Grier and Albin [1973] use intradaily data and examine returns from the time of the sale of the block of shares to the end of the day. Both studies find a reversal in prices following the sale. In other words, prices dropped with the sale of the block of shares and then partially rose by the end of the day. On the surface, these results suggest a market inefficiency because a trading strategy could be adopted to make abnormal returns. An additional analysis of these results by Carey [1977] and by Dann, Mayers, and Raab [1977] indicates that these abnormal returns could only be obtained for a very short time period following the sale of a block of shares. Within 5 to 10 minutes, any chance of making abnormal profits vanishes. This implies that there is an opportunity for specialists and floor traders to take advantage of market inefficiencies. But by the time outside investors receive the information about a block trade, the opportunity to make abnormal returns is past.

Hess and Frost [1982] examine price effects surrounding the issuance of new shares of an existing security. They conclude that these new issues cause neither a permanent nor temporary price effect.

The studies of price-pressure effects of block trades or the issuance of new securities provide estimates of how rapidly prices adjust to a sudden infusion of securities into the market. The 5-to-10-minute period of adjustment is short, but it demonstrates that perfect market efficiency is difficult, if not impossible, to obtain under existing market structures.

3.2.3 Dividend Announcements

The effect of dividends on the value of securities has been the center of an ongoing debate since Miller and Modigliani [1961] suggested the irrelevance of dividends in a world without taxes. But dividends to individuals are taxed and at rates higher than capital gains. This raises the question of why firms pay dividends instead of reinvesting earnings and generating capital gains. A possible explanation is that dividends are used to convey information from management to investors. Another possibility is that investors do not really pay higher taxes on dividends than they do on capital gains. Miller and Scholes [1978] demonstrate how individuals may avoid paying higher taxes on dividends. Moreover, the market may be dominated by nonindividual investors, such as corporations and trust funds, which are taxed at different rates, and who prefer dividends because of legal constraints on the separation of principal and income.

These explanations of the use of dividends have direct and indirect implications for the EMH. If dividends have information content, then price effects should be observed on the announcement date of dividends. If the EMH holds, then prices should quickly adjust to this new information and no further abnormal returns should occur following the announcement. The effect of taxes should be observed on the ex-dividend day (the day that determines who receives the dividends). If there were no taxes, then the EMH suggests that prices should drop by the amount of the dividend after adjusting for the expected return. Finally, the influence of taxes on dividends may affect the pricing model that is appropriate for the testing of the EMH. The use of an after-tax pricing model in this regard is discussed further in Chapter 5.

An early test of the EMH with respect to dividend announcements is due to Petit [1972]. He finds that prices adjust within a day of the dividend announcement except for announcements of initial dividends. Following the announcement of initial dividends, an investor could obtain a 16 percent abnormal return over the next 12 months. In a more recent study, Charest [1978b] uses monthly data to demonstrate abnormally high returns over 24 months following dividend increases and abnormally low returns over 24 months following dividend decreases. Charest, using daily data, also observes a similar drift in prices following an abrupt change in prices on the announcement date of a dividend change. Aharony and Itzhak [1980], however, examine the 10 days following dividend change announcements and observe no abnormal returns following the announcement date.

These dividend announcement date studies indicate that the market reacts rapidly to news about dividend changes, but there seems to be some long-term effects that are inconsistent with market efficiency. A possible explanation is the use of an inappropriate pricing model. Perhaps the dividend change coincides with a change in the pricing model that is not captured by the CAPM.

The existence of investors in different tax brackets creates a dilemma in defining market efficiency. This problem can be illustrated using the ex-dividend date. Elton and Gruber [1970] find that the average drop in price on the ex-dividend day is 78 percent of the size of the dividend. The failure of prices to reflect the full dividend is explained by the difference between ordinary and capital gains tax rates. But not all investors pay taxes. For example, pension funds pay no taxes on dividends. These results appear to offer the nontaxpaying investors an opportunity to buy the security just before the ex-dividend day, receive the untaxed dividend, and make an abnormal return. With diverse tax rates, abnormal returns are available to some investors. Whether these investors can take advantage of their tax status, however, depends on the transaction costs and the size of the potential profit.

The previous discussion is related to cash dividends. The issuance of stock dividends may also have price effects. Foster and Vickrey [1978] find that stock dividends have information content in that prices tended to rise with the announcement of a stock dividend. Because stock dividends are not taxable, however, the drop in price on the ex-dividend date should be equivalent to the dilutive effect of the increased number of shares. Foster and Vickrey [1978] observe that the market efficiently adjusts to stock dividends on the ex-dividend date, but Woolridge [1983] finds that prices do not drop sufficiently to account for stock dividends of 6 percent or less. This latter result is either inconsistent with semistrong market efficiency or it may once again indicate a misspecified pricing model.

3.2.4 Macroeconomic Factors

Present value analysis suggests a relationship between stock prices and interest rates. Interest rates are used to discount future cash flows to determine value. Indeed, Waud [1970] finds that stock prices change with announcements of changes in the Federal Reserve discount rate. Prices decreased with an increase in the discount rate and increased with a decrease in the discount rate. Observing a simultaneous change in stock prices and macroeconomic variables is not necessarily inconsistent with the EMH. However, if macroeconomic variables can be used to predict future stock prices and a viable trading rule can be established based on those predictions, then the EMH (conditional on the appropriate pricing model) can be rejected. This has not yet been done.

Monetary growth, which is related to interest rates through macroeconomic theory, has also been used in past studies to predict future stock price indices. But the ability to predict future stock price indices is not sufficient to reject the EMH. As mentioned in the discussion of weak-form market efficient tests, market indices may have nonzero serial correlation (allowing the use of past prices to predict future prices) and still be efficient. A market inefficiency is determined by the ability to earn a return beyond a market risk-adjusted return. Therefore, a trading strategy using financial instruments other than stocks is necessary to demonstrate market inefficiency.

Homa and Jaffee [1971] use predictions of the money supply to make predictions of the Standard & Poor's 500 stock index. Using this prediction model, they are able to establish a trading rule using either the S&P index or Treasury bills to obtain a higher return than a buy-and-hold strategy.

Their research, however, is criticized and restudied by others [Malkiel and Quandt, 1972; Pesando, 1974; Cooper, 1974; and Rozeff, 1974], who are critical of their failure to use a holdout sample for prediction purposes. These critics noted that the observed relationship between monetary growth and stock prices is unstable over time. The predictive power of these models on a holdout sample is found to be either nonexistent or small. In addition, attempts to find a trading strategy using the money supply to generate abnormal returns are unsuccessful, which is consistent with the EMH.

3.2.5 Exchange Market Information and Characteristics

Most market efficiency studies investigate price reactions to new information. Information about the trading behavior of other investors, however, should also be rapidly reflected in the prices. For example, the knowledge of the number of shares held short should not provide information that yields abnormal returns. But Figlewski [1981] notes that there is an inverse relationship between short interests and returns over the subsequent 12 months. In other words, a large (small) number of shares held short implies a lower (higher) return for a security in the next year. These results are obtained with, and hence conditional on, the CAPM being the correct pricing model.

Another stock market event that is used to test for market efficiency is the suspension of trading for a security. A trading suspension can be requested by the specialist when there is an imbalance between supply and demand, or, alternatively, an exchange may impose a suspension because of an impending or actual announcement that could have a significant impact on the stock price. Complete dissemination of the information is encouraged before the security is traded again. Hopewell and Schwartz [1976, 1978] find that the market reacts efficiently to trading suspensions. When the stock market reopens, there are no opportunities to make abnormal returns during the following days. Kryzanowski [1979], however, observed that the market does not completely adjust to trading suspensions caused by bad news. Prices continued to decline for 5 to 10 weeks following the reopening of trading on the suspended securities. Kryzanowski does find that the market reacts efficiently to trading suspensions associated with good news. He attributes this imbalance in market efficiency to restrictions on short sales.

A further stock market event that has received considerable attention is the initial issuance of the securities of a firm. These new issues are normally handled by underwriters who sell the securities at a set price. McDonald and Fisher [1972] and Ibbotson [1975] conclude that abnormally high returns are received by the initial subscribers to the security, but the market price adjusts within a week. The high return to the initial subscribers may be caused by underwriters selling securities at a discount to ensure that all the shares can be sold. Access to the market for new issues, however, is limited.

3.2.6 Firm Size and Year-end Tax Effects

A paper by Banz [1981] yields the surprising result that small firms tend to have higher abnormal returns than do larger firms. The profitability of buying securities of small firms is a phenomenon that has occurred over many years. The ability to make abnormal returns using an investment strategy based on size is inconsistent with semi-strong-form market efficiency since the size of the firm is information that is available to all investors.

Initial attempts to explain the *small-firm effect* involve a reexamination of the pricing model. Roll [1981] suggests that the systematic risk is measured incorrectly because of the infrequent trading of securities of small firms. Since returns are measured using the price of the last trade of the day, the time of that last trade is important in measuring returns. Scholes and Williams [1977] demonstrate that infrequent trading leads to a downward-biased measure of systematic risk. Reinganum [1982], however, finds that a misestimation of systematic risk in the market model could not completely explain the abnormal returns for small firms. Reinganum [1981a] also attempts to explain the small-firm effect through the use of an arbitrage pricing model, but without success. Small firms still made abnormal returns after adjusting raw returns with an arbitrage pricing model.

A study by Keim [1983] discovers that 50 percent of the annual small-firm effect took place in January and 25 percent of the small-firm effect took place during the first week of January. In another study, Roll [1983] finds that the 5 days of the year with the largest returns for all securities included the last trading day of December and the first 4 trading days of January. This propensity for large positive returns at the turn of the year would appear to be indicative of a tax effect rather than a risk measurement problem.

A tax effect could occur because of selling pressure on certain securities at the end of the year. This selling pressure occurs with firms that have depreciated in value and allows investors to recognize a capital loss, which investors should choose to take before the end of the year. At the beginning of the next year, the prices should rebound when this selling pressure is released. The problem with this hypothesis is that other investors should invest in these securities to the extent necessary to remove any abnormal returns.

The empirical tests performed to date indicate that a tax effect exists and that it is related to the small-firm effect. Dyl [1977] observes that securities that are losers in the previous 12 months tend to trade more in December than do securities that are winners. This is consistent with investors selling securities for tax purposes. Branch [1977] notes that those firms that have 12-month lows at the end of the year tend to rebound in January, indicating that selling pressure may be influencing prices. Roll [1983] and Givoly and Ovadia [1983] note that much of the small-firm effect in January occurred with firms that had losses in the previous year, especially when the

12- or 24-month low occurred in December. Both studies argue that the apparent selling pressure, which is predominant in smaller firms, is caused by the higher volatility of stock prices. Volatile securities are more likely to generate large losses and be candidates for selling to generate tax losses. These papers do not, however, explain all of the small-firm effect, especially during the rest of the year. Reinganum [1983] found that small firms with securities that appreciated in price the previous year still had abnormally high returns in January. Indeed, Brown, Keim, Kleidon, and Marsh [1983] observe abnormally high returns (especially in January) for small firms in Australia, even though the Australian tax year ends in June.

Several alternative hypotheses have been offered to explain the small-firm effect. Klein and Bawa [1977] model portfolio choice with different levels of security information. They note that risk-averse investors are more likely to invest in securities that they have more closely analyzed. Securities about which they have little information may be bypassed if the uncertainty about them is sufficiently large to overcome any perceived benefits of diversification. Arbel and Strebel [1983] suggest that this reluctance to invest in securities that are not well-known would necessitate a higher return for these securities to compensate for the uncertainty. This argument is inconsistent with the CAPM because only nondiversifiable risk should be rewarded, but Arbel and Strebel find that firms that are not closely followed by analysts (which they call "neglected firms") have higher returns than do closely analyzed securities, after controlling for size. These results indicate that the CAPM is incomplete or misspecified and that another risk factor related to information availability should be considered.

Another possible explanation of the small-firm effect is the higher transaction costs that must be incurred in buying securities of smaller firms. The higher transaction costs occur because securities that are traded less frequently (namely, smaller firms) tend to have higher bid-ask spreads. The higher bid-ask spread increases the cost of transacting in a security and reduces the marketability of that security. Investors would demand a higher return for this reduced marketability. Stoll and Whaley [1983] establish that for holding periods of less than one year, the transaction costs of buying small New York Stock Exchange (NYSE) firms are greater, on average, than are the returns from buying large NYSE firms. Schultz [1983], using American Stock Exchange (ASE) firms, finds significant returns after transaction costs for periods as short as a month, especially if that month included January.

The research to date indicates that there may be multiple reasons for the small-firm effect. There is also an indication that the small-firm effect is related to other instances of apparent market inefficiency. Reinganum [1981] and Basu [1983] both observe a relationship between price/earnings ratios and the size of the firms. The next chapter examines studies that suggest that a profitable strategy is to invest in securities with lower price/earnings ratios. The omission of common factors from the pricing model may explain most if not all of these divergencies from market efficiency.

3.2.7 Second-Hand Information

Most of the tests of semistrong market efficiency examine returns following some information announcement. The test is consistent with the EMH if the stock prices adjust quickly to the new information. Therefore, the EMH allows essentially no time for financial analysts to digest the raw information and provide advice (secondhand information) that will generate abnormal returns. Several studies, however, indicate that stock markets do react to announcements of financial analysts.

Value Line has consistently made recommendations that have provided followers of that financial service with abnormal returns. That result is documented by Black [1973] and by Copeland and Mayers [1982].

Changes in financial analyst forecasts of future earnings also apparently lead to abnormal returns. Givoly and Lakonishok [1979] find positive abnormal returns for up to two months following upward revisions in forecasts. Negative abnormal returns occur following downward revisions in forecasts.

The stock market also reacts sharply on the day of publication to articles on specific firms. Davies and Canes [1978] document large price reactions to financial analyst recommendations in "Heard on the Street" in *The Wall Street Journal*. Foster [1979] notes that securities prices drop an average of 8 percent following exposes by Abraham Briloff (e.g., Briloff, 1968, 1974) on the accounting methods of certain firms.

A final example of a stock market reaction to secondhand information centers on the announcement of the Consumer Price Index (CPI). Although the CPI is generated from prices available in the previous month, Schwert [1981] observes the stock market to react negatively to the announcement of unexpected inflation.

These results are particularly troublesome to those who maintain that the EMH is descriptive of the securities market. An argument can be made that analysts have access to private information, but that implies that the market is strong-form inefficient. A misspecified pricing model could also explain long-term abnormal returns, but it would not explain price reactions on the day of analyst announcements.

3.3 TESTS OF STRONG-FORM MARKET EFFICIENCY

A market that is strong-form efficient exhibits prices that not only reflect public information but also private information. Such a market is also weak-form and semistrong-form efficient. Different scenarios that allow prices to reflect private information are presented in Chapter 2. Whether those mechanisms for price adjustment cause prices to reflect private information rapidly is an empirical question.

The problem with testing strong-form market efficiency is that private information, by its nature, is unobservable. Therefore, indirect methods must be used to test for strong-form market efficiency. Researchers have examined portfolio returns likely to reflect private information, such as mutual funds and the returns earned by insiders as defined by the Securities and Exchange Commission (SEC). If abnormally high returns are found, then an argument can be made that prices do not reflect the private information that the investors have.

Another indirect approach to testing for strong-form market efficiency is to examine returns and trading volume prior to public announcements. Certain types of return and trading behavior are consistent with the use of private information, but other scenarios could also explain the results.

3.3.1 Tests of Mutual Fund Performance

Many mutual fund managers spend a great deal of money to improve their funds' investment performance. Analysts for mutual funds interview corporate managers and dig through trade journals, SEC reports, and other information sources that the average investor cannot obtain at a reasonable cost. If these information sources represent private information and a trading strategy is implemented using this information, then examining the returns of mutual funds offers an opportunity to test strong-form market efficiency.

Several researchers have examined the performance of mutual funds [Sharpe, 1966; Jensen, 1968; and Kon and Jen, 1979]. The results of their work indicate that mutual funds do not achieve abnormally high returns on average. In addition, Schlarbaum, Lewellen, and Lease [1978] examined portfolio decisions of individual investors. These individual investors achieved returns that are comparable to mutual fund returns even though they probably used fewer resources in gathering their information.

The inability of mutual funds to make abnormal returns may be due to their inability to obtain private information. To the extent that these mutual funds gather, analyze, and use information, however, the stock market appears to provide no returns beyond those expected by the market model.

3.3.2 Trading By Insiders

Insiders are defined by the SEC as directors, managers, and owners of at least 10 percent of the shares of the firm. Restrictions are imposed on the trading of these insiders. Insiders cannot sell short and must return to the firm any profit made on shares held for less than 6 months. Insiders are also not supposed to trade on private information, although regulation of this type of trading is difficult. In addition, insiders must report all their transactions in their firm's securities to the SEC. The SEC publishes these transactions each month in the *Official Summary*.

The *Official Summary* has been used as a data base for testing whether insiders earn abnormal returns. The most common approach is to create portfolios each month based on the number of insiders purchasing and selling the security that month. Lorie and Niederhoffer [1968], Jaffe [1974a], and Finnerty [1976] have all demonstrated that purchasing a security during months when more insiders purchase than sell and selling a security during months when more insiders sell than purchase yields a trading strategy with abnormally high returns. Using a trading strategy based on the number of shares purchased and sold by insiders, however, does not produce abnormally high returns. These studies seem to indicate that insiders have information that is not impounded in prices, but it is not clear whether as a group they are taking advantage of this information.

Information about insider trading becomes public information through the *Official Summary* up to 5 or 6 weeks following the actual transaction of the insider. But Jaffe [1974a] also demonstrates that a trading strategy based on the number of insider buyers and sellers generated abnormal returns after the publication date of the *Official Summary*.

Jaffe [1974b] also notes that the trading strategy using the number of insider buyer and sellers is successful during different time periods. Since abnormally high returns continued in spite of well-publicized cases against insiders, trading on private information, sanctions do not seem to limit trading by insiders.

Penman [1982] examined insider trading around a specific information event, namely, a firm's voluntary forecast of future earnings. He discovered that insiders tended to purchase shares before the announcement and sell their shares after the announcement. Given that earnings forecasts are generally positively received by the market, insiders are able to make abnormal returns by adjusting their trading around the announcement.

Although insiders are prohibited from using private information to trade in securities, they appear to have information that is not impounded in the stock price. Further research is necessary to learn more about the use of this information by insiders.

3.3.3 Using Price Changes and Trading Volume to Make Inferences About the Use of Private Information

Tests of the semistrong form of market efficiency generally examine returns that are available following a certain type of information announcement. In some cases there is considerable price reaction preceding the announcement. This price reaction is often attributed to *leaks* of the information through other information sources. Whether these "leaks" are in the form of public information announcements or occur through private channels is unclear.

Morse [1980] argues that one method of attempting to discriminate between price reactions caused by public information and price reactions caused by private information is through examining trading volume. If public information is released and investors' beliefs change uniformly given the information, then prices will adjust rapidly with little trading. If, however, a small group of investors receives the information first, they will trade until the price adjusts to reflect the information. This is the speculative behavior discussed in Chapter 2. Therefore, the argument goes, information that is disseminated privately leads to greater trading volume than does information released publicly. Morse also suggests that a monotonic movement of prices should be observed when prices are adjusting to private information.

Morse [1980] observes greater than normal trading the day before large price changes. He also observes that periods of greater than normal trading volume are accompanied by monotonic changes in prices. Both of these results are consistent with successful trading on private information.

Keown and Pinkerton [1981] observe a similar price/volume reaction before merger announcements. Abnormally high returns and high trading volume occur 2 to 3 weeks prior to the public announcement.

Abdel-khalik and Ajinkya [1982] establish that high returns are available the week before analyst earnings announcements. These forecasts are formulated and known by a small group of individuals prior to their announcement, but prices do not reflect this information until it is publicly announced.

These results also suggest that the market is not strong-form efficient. Prices do not appear to adjust completely to information held by a small number of investors.

3.4 TESTS OF PRICE VARIANCES
AND OVERREACTION TO INFORMATION

An entirely different approach to testing for market efficiency has recently been introduced. Shiller [1981a] and LeRoy and Porter [1981] demonstrate that stock prices have much higher variances than would be implied by the past time series of dividends and earnings. One possible explanation of this result is that investors are overreacting to information and therefore market prices do not reflect the available information.

The method used by Shiller [1981a] and LeRoy and Porter [1981] is to generate a past price series based on a present value model. The inputs to the present value model include actual past dividends or earnings and a constant discount rate. The past price series generated by the present value model has a much smaller variance than does the actual price series.

One possible explanation of these results is that the discount rate varies over time, which would cause the price series to vary even more. Shiller [1981b], however, demonstrates that the discount rate would have to vary at an unreasonably high level to explain the results. Another possible explanation tested by Shiller [1981b] is the failure to allow for a major catastrophe in the dividend series used in the present value model. If the subjective probability of a major catastrophe occurring changes over time, then the generated price series would exhibit greater variance. But, once again, this explanation is not sufficient to explain the extreme results obtained by Shiller.

Another possible explanation is that the present value model may not be appropriate. LeRoy and La Civita [1981] demonstrate that with unrestricted probability distributions, the present value model will only be appropriate under risk neutrality. LeRoy and La Civita [1981] and Michener [1982] point out that price variability increases with increased risk aversion of investors. This result could explain the low variance generated from the present value model.

Although tests of price variance offer an alternative approach to testing market efficiency, the approach still suffers from a need for a pricing model. In addition, no direct tests of a trading strategy have been performed. Presumably this type of test would need to be the opposite of the filter-type test to take advantage of the overreaction of prices to information.

3.5 ARBITRAGE OPPORTUNITIES

Arbitrage opportunities occur when an investor can make a certain positive return with no investment. Such arbitrage opportunities may be available when multiple securities exist related to the same underlying assets. There is a relationship among the prices of these securities that can be determined if the distribution of the future returns of the underlying assets is known. If the expected pricing relationship is not observed, then either the future return distribution is misspecified or an arbitrage opportunity exists. The existence of an arbitrage opportunity is inconsistent with the EMH because an infinite return can be obtained based on a zero investment. Transaction costs, such as brokerage fees, and constraints on borrowing and short selling, limit these arbitrage opportunities.

The best known pricing relationship is the *option pricing model*. An option pricing model relates the prices of stock, options, and debt. Black and Scholes [1973] developed an option pricing model by assuming that stock prices follow a specified diffusion process.

Manaster and Rendleman [1982] use the *Black-Scholes model* to test whether option prices contain any information about stock prices. Their results suggest that some securities are overpriced while other securities are underpriced. (This finding may be due, however, to a misspecification of the Black-Scholes model.) Manaster and Rendleman took the analysis one step farther by looking at the stock returns for the days following the determination of the implied prices from the Black-Scholes model. They find that stocks with prices greater than the implied prices from the Black-Scholes model performed worse than did stocks with prices less than the implied price. These results suggest that there is information in option prices that is not immediately reflected in the stock price. Manaster and Rendleman credit option markets with being more efficient than stock markets because of lower transaction costs.

Another form of an apparent arbitrage opportunity is the existence of discounts and premiums for shares of closed-end mutual funds. A discount or premium occurs when the market value of the shares held by the fund differs from the market value of the fund's shares. If a discount on the fund's shares exists, then all the shares of the fund should be purchased to obtain the more valuable securities held by the fund. With a premium, an investor should sell the fund's shares and buy the individual securities in the open market.

Thompson [1978] determined that closed-end mutual funds do better than the market following the existence of a discount and worse than the market following the existence of a premium. These results are consistent with temporary market inefficiencies for the shares of closed-end mutual funds.

3.6 TAKEOVERS AND MERGERS

The EMH states that the share price of a firm reflects all the information about the value of the firm. One group of investors that apparently does not believe in the EMH is the management of corporations that purchase other corporations for an amount above the existing share price. These purchases may be in the form of a tender offer or a merger agreement that offers a premium to the shareholders of the acquired corporation. If a corporation pays a premium for the shares of another corporation, then the EMH suggests that the acquiring corporation is paying too much. To compensate for purchasing an overpriced good, the market should penalize the acquiring firm by reducing its share price.

The empirical work by Mandelker [1974] and Asquith and Kim [1982] shows that acquired-firm shareholders profit from the merger while there is no effect on the wealth of the acquiring-firm shareholders. Bradley [1980] observes that the average premium paid with tender offers is 49 percent over the price 2 months before the acquisition. Because the acquiring firm's share price does not drop, the premium paid cannot be explained as a managerial mistake.

A common explanation for the joint value of two corporations being greater together than apart is synergy. Synergy could occur because of reduced production or distribution costs when the firms are operated jointly. But this potential synergy must have existed some time before the acquisition. Why didn't these acquisitions take place when prices first created these synergistic advantages and why didn't the price of the acquired firm reflect the potential for acquisition instead of adjusting when the takeover becomes imminent or announced? These questions remain unanswered.

Another possible explanation of the large premium that acquiring firms are willing to pay is the discovery of private information that the target firm is undervalued. Dodd and Ruback [1977], Bradley [1980], and Dodd [1980] observe that unsuccessful attempts to takeover or merge left the target firm with a higher share price than before the takeover or merger attempt. These results are consistent with the revelation of private information through the acquisition attempt. The stock market is apparently inefficient with respect to the private information before the acquisition attempt, but it becomes efficient when the acquisition attempt takes place. This explanation would be consistent with a strong-form inefficiency.

Neither explanation of the premium paid to target firms is consistent with the EMH. If synergies exist, they are only reflected in the price when an acquisition takes place. The market does not appear to adjust for the potential for synergistic combinations. The private information explanation, on the other hand, is based on strong-form market inefficiency. In either case, the abnormal returns appear to be too large and occur over too short a time period to be explained by a misspecified pricing model.

Still one other possible explanation rests on the statistical nature of the EMH. The EMH should not be expected to hold in every case. It represents the norm, but exceptions are bound to exist. The cases cited may simply be these exceptions.

3.7 USING EXPERIMENTAL MARKETS TO TEST FOR MARKET EFFICIENCY

One of the problems with testing for informational efficiency in securities markets is the inability of observing the "correct" price. If the "correct" price could be observed, then it could be compared with the actual price and the question of market efficiency readily resolved.

With experimental markets, the opportunity exists to establish markets for securities with predetermined economic values. The question addressed in these studies is whether trading among the participants takes place at a price equal to the economic value of the security. These experimental markets are normally repeated to determine the rapidity of the convergence of transaction prices.

Two recent studies using experimental market focus on the issue of market efficiency. In Forsythe, Palfrey, and Plott [1982], a two-period market is established involving a single security. The security pays different levels of dividends to participants in each of the two periods, but the participants do not know the dividends to be received by other investors. Knowledge of everyone's dividends could be used to determine the value of the security. Although several repetitions are required before prices converge, the resultant price is almost identical to the predetermined value using all the dividend information in the market. This implies that the participants are able to obtain information from transaction prices.

Plott and Sunder [1982] established an experimental market with certain individuals given private information about the value of the securities. They find that other participants are rapidly able to discern the information through the prices. After several repetitions, the privately informed participants are not able to earn significantly higher returns than the uninformed participants.

These experimental market studies provide evidence that securities markets may be very efficient, even with respect to private information. Prices appear to convey information to the uninformed. Although these experimental markets are only simple representations of actual securities markets, they do demonstrate that mechanisms exist that can cause securities markets to be efficient.

3.8 SUMMARY

Prices in a perfectly efficient market fully reflect all information and adjust immediately to new information. This is an extreme standard and impossible to attain because stocks do not trade continually. Therefore, prices cannot be updated immediately. The research reviewed in this chapter attempts to determine the degree of market efficiency found in the stock market. The results are still joint tests of market efficiency and a pricing model, but certain results are less sensitive to the misspecification of the pricing model.

The studies reviewed in this chapter seem to indicate that the stock market is weak-form efficient. Attempts to develop a superior trading strategy using the serial correlation of returns, filter rules, or return cycles are unsuccessful.

The results relating market efficiency to public information are less clear. Long-term abnormal returns appear to be available after certain information events and are based on specific exchange and firm characteristics. Whether these returns are a function of a misspecified pricing model or not is unclear. This issue is examined again in Chapter 5.

The speed of price adjustments appears to be very rapid. Some tests indicate that the market price adjusts within 5 to 10 minutes. But the market also appears to react to some events that could be considered "secondhand information." The analysis of information that is already publicly available sometimes generates further price reactions.

The studies reviewed in this chapter cast serious doubt on the efficiency of the market with respect to private information. Insiders appear to have information that is not fully reflected in prices. Prices adjust in a manner consistent with the use of private information prior to a public announcement. Takeover bids seem to be motivated, at least in part, by private information that is not reflected in the stock's price.

Other tests also cast doubt on complete market efficiency. Stock prices seem to vary more than expected and trading strategies based on arbitrage opportunities appear to generate unexpected returns. On the other hand, experimental markets in laboratory settings yield results consistent with the ability of markets to attain prices that reflect the value of the security. These studies and others leave the issue of market efficiency based on nonaccounting information an open question.

CHAPTER FOUR

Tests of Market Efficiency Using Accounting Information

Accounting reports detail the financial activities and status of a firm. Accounting information is derived through application of a rather specific and detailed set of rules that relies heavily on historical costs. Earnings figures generated through the accounting process, therefore, do not (nor are they designed to) represent the change in value of the firm. Characteristics of accounting information are discussed in more detail in the first section of this chapter.

Although accounting earnings do not perfectly reflect the change in value of a firm, accounting numbers may be associated with the value of the firm. If so, they provide information relevant to the pricing of a firm's securities. Accounting numbers are also commonly used in management compensation contracts and in debt covenants. Uses of accounting information are discussed in the second section of this chapter.

The third section reviews studies that examine market reactions at the time of an accounting announcement. Large price changes and abnormally high trading volume when accounting announcements are released would be consistent with the use of accounting information by investors.

Tests of market efficiency using accounting information are primarily of the semistrong form. These tests generally examine the returns following an accounting announcement. The fourth section of this chapter examines tests of this type. Any abnormal returns found by these tests could also be interpreted as a misspecification of the pricing model rather than market efficiency.

Section 5 evaluates research based on the *price/earnings (P/E) ratio*. The P/E ratio is commonly used by financial analysts in evaluating a security. Studies using the P/E ratio to form an investment strategy are examined in this section.

The sixth section of this chapter looks at accounting changes. An accounting change can be mandated by either the Securities and Exchange Commission (SEC) or the Financial Accounting Standards Board (FASB). In other cases, the accounting change is discretionary. An accounting change usually alters the accounting numbers reported by a firm and may also change the actions of managers. Whether these accounting changes affect investor evaluations is an empirical question that has implications for the EMH. If the market price is affected by a change in accounting method that has no economic (including informational) effect, then the market would be inefficient with respect to the specific item in question.

4.1 CHARACTERISTICS OF ACCOUNTING INFORMATION

The SEC requires corporations whose securities are traded on organized exchanges to issue quarterly reports every 3 months and an annual report following the end of the firm's fiscal year. These reports are intended to be financial summaries of the activities of the corporation in the previous period. The rules for generating these accounting reports, however, are often complex and may even appear at times to disguise the financial welfare of the corporation. Therefore, a brief review of the basic rules and characteristics of accounting is useful in interpreting studies examining stock market reactions to accounting reports.

Accounting reports are based on historical cost systems. Assets are recorded at their original cost less any accrued depreciation, depletion, or amortization. Although large corporations are required at this time to provide some supplementary current value data, the basic financial statements typically make no effort to report changes in the value of the assets held by the corporation. Revaluation of an asset only takes place when it is purchased or sold. Therefore, these financial reports make no systematic attempt to reflect changes in the value of the corporation.

The earnings in accounting reports differ from economic earnings, which are defined in terms of changes in value. Accounting earnings rely instead on the principles of realization and matching. Revenues are considered realized when a product is sold or a service is provided regardless of when the money is received. Expenditures are matched to revenues if they are considered as helping to generate those revenues. Otherwise, costs are treated as assets to be written off in the future. Matching results in the choice of arbitrary methods to allocate joint production costs to products and to allocate costs among different time periods. The difference between these revenues and allocated costs (called expenses) is defined as accounting earnings and could be considerably different from economic earnings.

To reduce the arbitrariness of the choice of allocational methods, regulatory bodies have constrained the accounting options of corporations. Their objective in part is to help ensure consistency between years and comparability among firms. The SEC and the Financial Accounting Standards Board (FASB), which was preceded by the Accounting Principles Board (APB), have issued pronouncements concerning which accounting methods firms must use for reporting purposes if their securities trade publicly. In many cases, however, corporations are still free to make a choice between several alternative accounting methods. For example, firms can choose between straight-line and several accelerated methods of depreciation.

Another characteristic of accounting reports is that they are not usually timely. Accounting reports are issued every 3 months. Between accounting reports many events affecting the firm occur. These events may be disclosed initially through newspaper articles or trade journals or by investment brokers. These alternative sources of information often usurp some or all of the information value in accounting reports. Moreover, there is a considerable delay between the end of the accounting period and publication of the report reflecting the financial results for that period.

4.2 USE OF ACCOUNTING INFORMATION

Disclosure of accounting information is required by the SEC to allow investors to make intelligent portfolio decisions. Exactly how an investor should use accounting information to make investment decisions is, however, unclear. Present value analysis would suggest that the discounting of future cash flows should be used to determine value. But future cash flows are uncertain, and estimates of future cash flows are not provided in accounting reports. Other valuation formulas tend to be without any theoretical underpinnings. Using accounting numbers to determine underpriced or overpriced securities is an art, not a science. Indeed, the EMH implies that it is impossible consistently to select underpriced or overpriced securities.

Accounting data may also provide investors with information about the riskiness of a security. Beaver, Kettler, and Scholes [1970] observe significant associations of market-determined risk measures with accounting estimates of risk. Therefore, accounting information may allow investors to choose securities that match their risk preferences. Chapter 6 contains a more detailed discussion of the implications of the EMH for the use of accounting information by investors.

Accounting numbers can also be used by noninvestors. One example is the use of accounting numbers by managers to make more efficient production decisions. Also managers' compensation may be based partially on accounting numbers. Banks use accounting information to make credit decisions. Government units use accounting information to impose taxes and enforce other regulations. Each of these uses of accounting information and others as well may affect the value of the stock. Therefore, the relationship between accounting numbers and stock prices is complex.

4.3 MARKET REACTIONS
TO ACCOUNTING REPORTS

With the existence of other more timely information sources, whether the market would react at all to the issuance of an accounting report is unclear. If the accounting report contains no new information, the EMH would suggest that the market price should not change with the release of the report.

An early study of the relationship between prices and accounting reports is due to Ball and Brown [1968]. They look particularly at annual earnings numbers. Ball and Brown reason that market participants form opinions of what the earnings numbers should be, and, collectively, these opinions are reflected in a market forecast of the stock's price.

They further reason that the reaction of a stock's price reflects the difference between the firm's actual earnings and the market's forecast. Accordingly, Ball and Brown form estimates of the market's earnings forecast and then evaluate a security price reaction to good news (when actual earnings exceed the forecast) and to bad news (when actual earnings fall short of the forecast). The market reaction to unexpected earnings is measured as though the market participants had access to the good or bad news prior to the availability of this news to the market. Their measure accumulates and averages the excess return that could be made over the time period prior to the announcement date. In the case of good news, the average cumulative abnormal return begins to rise 12 months prior to the actual annual earnings announcement, due, it is presumed, to alternative sources of information such as interim reports. By the time of the announcement, the average excess return reaches about 7.5 percent. A mirror image of the same behavior is observed in the case of bad news, with the average cumulative abnormal return reaching 10 percent by the announcement date of annual earnings. Figure 4-1 illustrates Ball and Brown's findings for the good-news and bad-news cases.

Although there is a positive association between unexpected earnings and excess returns, most of the price response takes place

FIGURE 4-1

Abnormal performance indexes for various portfolios: Price behavior for stocks with good news and bad news. *Source:* Ball and Brown [1968], p. 169.

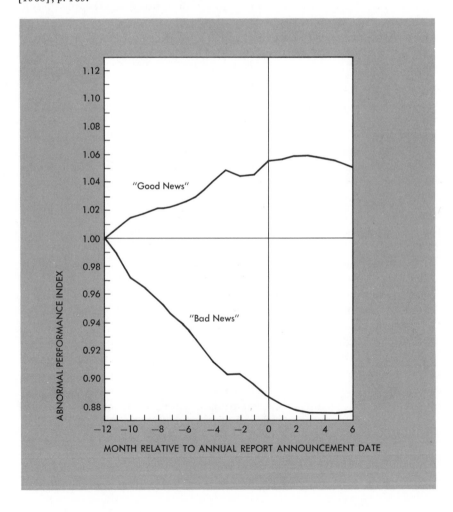

before the annual report is actually released. Ball and Brown estimate that only 10–15 percent of the market reaction takes place during the announcement month. Brown and Kennelly [1972] note similar results with quarterly earnings.

The Ball and Brown [1968] study seems to indicate very little price adjustment in the announcement month. Beaver [1968] uses an alternative approach to investigate the market's reaction to announcements of annual reports. Beaver examines the size of price changes and the levels of trading volume in the weeks surrounding the announcement of a firm's annual earnings in *The Wall Street Journal.* He finds that the absolute values of the price changes and the levels of trading were significantly higher during the announccement week than in any other week. In addition, price changes and volume in the week following the announcement week return to preannouncement levels. While this research does not provide any definitive conclusions concerning the lack of bias in the market's assessment of new information, it does provide substantive evidence that the reaction occurs quickly, one of the characteristics of market efficiency. Figures 4-2 and 4-3 summarize Beaver's results on price

FIGURE 4-2

Price residual analysis. *Source:* Beaver [1968], p. 91.

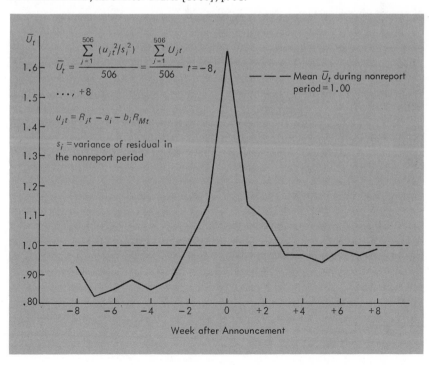

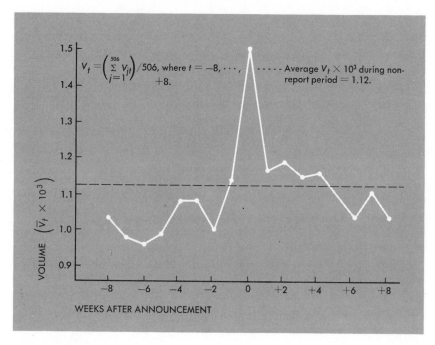

FIGURE 4-3

Volume stock trading. *Source:* Beaver [1968], p. 89.

and volume reaction to annual reports. May [1971] and Kiger [1972] observe similar results surrounding the release of quarterly earnings.

Morse [1981] also studies the market reaction to accounting reports using daily data. He observes large price reactions to accounting reports for two days following *The Wall Street Journal* announcement and unusual trading volume during the three days following the announcement. Therefore, while the market responds quickly, there appears to be some delay before the market settles down following the release of an accounting report.

Patell and Wolfson [1979, 1981] discover that investors antici-pate a price reaction to accounting reports. The authors were able to derive this result by using the relationship between option and stock prices. The variance of the stock price influences the option price. By using the option price, Patell and Wolfson are able to determine the implied variance of the stock price. Prior to the announcement of accounting reports, option prices increased implying that investors anticipated a higher stock price variance with the release of the accounting report.

The price reaction to accounting reports appears to be greater for smaller firms. Grant [1980] finds that firms traded over-the-counter, which tend to be smaller, have greater price reactions to accounting reports than do New York Stock Exchange firms. He attributes the greater price reaction for accounting reports of smaller firms to fewer alternative information sources. More timely alternative information sources would also usurp some of the information content of accounting reports.

The results from all these studies seem to indicate that investors do use accounting information. Market prices adjust rapidly, but not instantaneously, to the information in accounting reports. Much of the information in the accounting reports, however, has already reached the market through alternative sources. Given that the information in accounting reports is a financial summary of events that occurred in a prior period, it is not surprising that some price adjustments are made before the announcement. Information in accounting reports could be considered "secondhand" information because all the events reflected by the accounting have already taken place. If true, any price reaction to accounting reports is at the least inconsistent with strong-form market efficiency. An alternative explanation is that the accounting process applied to the raw information events creates new information. The next section reviews accounting reports and semistrong-form market efficiency by examining returns following the announcement of accounting reports.

4.4 TESTS OF RETURNS FOLLOWING ACCOUNTING ANNOUNCEMENTS

Under semistrong market efficiency, abnormal returns cannot be made through the use of public information. Once accounting reports are released, the semistrong form of the EMH states that no trading strategies using the accounting report exist that consistently yield abnormal returns. Most of the trading strategies that have been tested using accounting reports involve the earnings figure. A common approach is to categorize earnings numbers as "good news" or "bad news" and then examine returns following the announcement of the earnings figure.

4.4.1 Use of the Earnings Number

The first test of semistrong market efficiency using accounting numbers is due to Ball and Brown [1968]. They observe that following the announcement of annual earnings, both "good" and "bad" earnings numbers are followed by approximately zero abnormal returns. This can be seen in Figure 4-1.

Subsequent studies of return behavior following the announcement of earnings figures yield conflicting results. The following articles report abnormal returns following annual or quarterly announcements, which is inconsistent with market efficiency: Jones and Litzenberger [1970]; Joy, Litzenberger, and McEnally [1977]; Brown [1978]; Watts [1978]; Latané and Jones [1979]; Nichols and Brown [1981]; and Rendleman, Jones, and Latané [1982]. These articles document positive abnormal returns for several months following large increases in earnings and negative abnormal returns for several months following large decreases in earnings. An example of these results can be seen in Figure 4-4 from Rendleman, Jones, and Latané [1982]. The most extreme earnings change groups have

FIGURE 4-4

Cumulative excess returns averaged over the 36-quarter period 1971 (3) to 1980 (2). *Source:* Rendleman et al. [1982], p. 285.

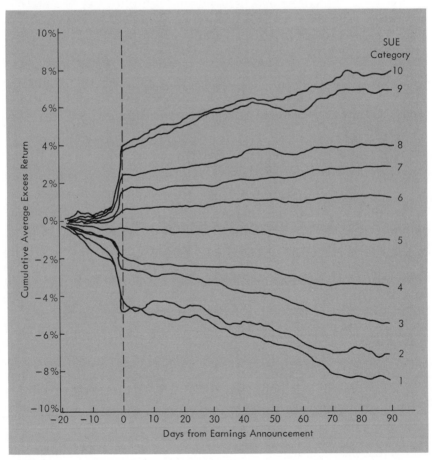

larger abnormal returns. Ball [1978] reviews additional articles with similar results.

Initial attempts to explain these results focused on experimental problems. For example, Joy, Litzenberger, and McEnally [1977] improve on Jones and Litzenberger [1970] by establishing the actual announcement date with greater accuracy. They also use reported earnings rather than revised earnings numbers, and they adjust data for bankrupt firms. None of these adjustments affected results.

Watts [1978] examines the effect of measurement errors on the coefficients of the market model. He concludes that the abnormal returns are too large to be explained by this potential source of measurement error. Watts also suggests that the market inefficiency occurs only during a certain time period [1962–1965], but Rendleman, Jones, and Latané [1982] found that the abnormal returns occurred throughout the 1970s. Therefore, the results could not be explained by experimental error during a single time period. Further, no apparent learning is taking place in the market given that the Jones and Litzenberger results were known in 1970.

Size of the abnormal returns and length of time they persist vary across studies and time periods investigated. Even when transaction costs are considered, abnormal returns are still available for traders on exchange floors and in many cases to outside investors. These abnormal returns occur up to 90 days following quarterly earnings announcements. The results suggest that the market does not react rapidly to new information, and there appears to be time for investors to take advantage of unexpected earnings information.

Ball [1978] observes that the remaining alternative explanation to market inefficiency is a misspecification of the pricing model. Ball points out that abnormal returns are more likely to occur with a misspecified model if sample firms tend to remain in the same portfolio categories in each time period. For example, if certain firms are always in the positive earnings change (good news) group and if these firms have common risk characteristics that are not specified in the pricing model that justify a higher return, then the positive earnings change group will consistently yield positive abnormal returns. For a preliminary study, Watts [1978] observed, however, that earnings changes are not highly correlated across time. Therefore, he concludes that model misspecification is less likely to be a problem because firms tend to move between positive and negative earnings change groups with equal probability across time. If a factor is omitted from the pricing model, it would have to change signs with the earnings change to cause the abnormal returns generated using the market model.

Latané and Jones [1979] provide further information that

allows us to speculate on whether abnormal returns following earnings announcements are due to a misspecification of the pricing model or to market inefficiency. They observe that during periods when the overall market is doing well, negative abnormal returns are more pronounced following a negative change in earnings. Also, during periods when the overall market is doing poorly, positive abnormal returns are more pronounced following a positive change in earnings. The abnormal return pattern following earnings announcements are more pronounced for smaller firms than for larger firms.

Separately these results do not allow differentiation between the model misspecification hypothesis and the inefficient market hypothesis, but the patterns related to general market movements combined with the results for smaller firms, which have already been determined to have a different return behavior, suggest that the market model is misspecified. Latané and Jones [1979] hypothesize that the abnormal returns that are available following earnings announcements by smaller firms may be due to market inefficiencies caused by a smaller following of analysts and investors.

A recent paper by Foster, Olsen, and Shevlin [1984] sheds some light on this unusual return behavior. They find that forming portfolios by quarterly earnings changes creates similar portfolios over time. As discussed earlier, Ball [1978] identified this characteristic as potentially causing abnormal returns when the pricing model is misspecified. Foster, Olsen, and Shevlin skirt this problem by using return residuals on the earnings announcement date to form portfolios. The composition of these portfolios tends to be independent over time. Using this method of forming portfolio yields no unusual return behavior following the earnings announcement and suggests again that the results of previous studies are caused by a misspecified pricing model.

4.4.2 Use of Other Information in the Accounting Report

Information other than the earnings number is released in an accounting report. Some studies have investigated whether the market reacts efficiently to this additional information. Most of these studies have focused on the effect of a change in accounting principles. These studies are reviewed in Section 4.6. Accounting reports also contain balance sheet data, footnotes, and audit reports that have been used to test for market efficiency.

Firth [1978] looks at the return effects of annual accounting reports with qualified audit opinions in the United Kingdom. He finds that stock prices drop sharply on the announcement date but that no subsequent abnormal returns could be obtained. Elliott

[1982] also documents insignificant abnormal returns subsequent to specific types of qualified opinions.

There have also been several studies of market efficiency that employ multiple variables from the accounting report. Altman [1968] estimates a model based on ratios derived from working capital, retained earnings, earnings, debt, and sales to predict bankruptcies. Altman and Brenner [1981] use this bankruptcy prediction model to choose firms that are likely to go bankrupt in the near future. They then test whether the market price reflects the increased probability of bankruptcy at the time of the announcement of the accounting report. The authors find that negative abnormal returns continue to occur up to 12 months subsequent to the announcement. One of the variables used in bankruptcy prediction models is earnings, so these negative abnormal returns may be related to the studies finding negative abnormal returns following an earnings decrease. Therefore, a misspecified pricing model could be the cause of these negative abnormal returns.

Graham [1973 and previous editions] attempts to provide a formula for investing using a number of criteria. He suggests investing in firms that provide consistent dividends, are among the *larger firms* in their respective industries, indicate debt-to-equity ratio of less than 1, and have a relatively low P/E ratio. Oppenheimer and Schlarbaum [1981] test this investment strategy and find that a positive abnormal return can be obtained. The potential driving force of these results could be the use of P/E ratios. Studies reviewed in the next section indicate that strategies using P/E ratios may yield abnormal returns when using the market model to specify normal returns.

4.5 TRADING STRATEGIES BASED ON P/E RATIOS

P/E ratios are commonly used by financial analysts, but their interpretation is unclear. Beaver and Morse [1978] among others have attempted to explain why P/E ratios vary among firms. Theory combining the present value formula and the CAPM suggests that the P/E ratio is a function of risk and future earnings growth. If some measure of permanent earnings is incorporated in the P/E ratio, then any variance of P/E ratios among firms should be caused only by risk differences across firms. But Beaver and Morse find that the cross-sectional variance of the P/E ratio cannot be explained solely by risk as measured by beta. They attribute much of the variance in P/E ratios to an earnings figure that contains transitory elements that do not affect the price of the security. For example, a high P/E ratio could be caused by a temporary decline in earnings while a low P/E ratio could be caused by a temporary rise in earnings. Therefore, any tests of market efficiency using P/E ratios should be related to tests of market efficiency following earnings announcements. As mentioned earlier, there is evidence that abnormal returns following earnings announcements are related to pricing model deficiencies.

Basu [1977, 1978] demonstrates that P/E ratios can be used to generate abnormal returns based on the market model. Firms with high P/E ratios tend to decline in price while firms with low P/E ratios tend to increase in price. While these results are inconsistent with market efficiency, they are consistent with the finding of abnormal returns following earnings changes.

Reinganum [1981b] also found that the use of P/E ratios leads to abnormal returns. In addition, he notes that small firms tended to have extreme P/E ratios. He concludes that the market inefficiency results using earnings changes, P/E ratios, and firm size are all related to a common omitted variable in the pricing model. Unfortunately, the variable remains, at present, unidentified.

4.6 MARKET EFFICIENCY AND CHANGES IN ACCOUNTING PRINCIPLES

As mentioned in Section 4.1, accounting numbers are based on complex rules or principles. These rules or principles may be changed by regulatory bodies or, in some cases, by the firm when a choice among principles is allowed. These changes in principles create different accounting numbers, and comparisons over time and between firms become more difficult. The confounding of information caused by changes in accounting principles may confuse investors and cause prices to react inefficiently by reflecting changes in accounting numbers rather than changes in the economic characteristics of the firm. Therefore, tests of price effects of accounting principle choices are often considered to be tests of market efficiency.

Early studies of this type used *earnings capitalization models* (which express security prices as a function of earnings). The simplest of these models states that price is a linear function of earnings or that the price/earnings ratio is constant. Tests performed by O'Donnell [1965, 1968] Mlynarczyk [1969], Gonedes [1969], Comiskey [1971], and Beaver and Dukes [1973] attempt to determine if the market capitalizes earnings differently under alternative accounting principles. For example, Comiskey [1971] notes that price/earnings ratios tended to drop when steel firms changed from accelerated depreciation to straight-line depreciation. Comiskey interpreted the result as the market discounting earnings numbers produced by a more liberal accounting policy. In other words, the market is not fooled by the accounting change and prices reacted efficiently to reflect the different accounting methods. Results consistent with market efficiency are generally found by this research.

There are several problems with these types of tests. As discussed in the previous section, price/earnings ratios may differ because of risk and other factors. Although the early studies of accounting changes often used a control group of firms with a different accounting principle, there is no guarantee that other factors that would affect the results are controlled. Indeed, the act of choosing different accounting principles may imply that the firms are substantively, perhaps economically, different. Firms with different economic profiles might be expected to select different accounting methods.

Another approach to examining the price effects of accounting principle changes is to look at returns surrounding the announcement of earnings with an accounting change. Ball [1972] performs such a study using a sample with a variety of different accounting changes. While Ball observes that the firms in his sample do experience changes in their risk characteristics, there is no evidence of an abnormal return in the months surrounding the accounting changes.

Although these initial studies found that prices compensated for differences in accounting methods and that no abnormal returns are observed when accounting changes are made, later studies began to question the hypothesis that no price reaction to an accounting change is consistent with market efficiency. Harrison [1977] points out that accounting changes mandated by the FASB or SEC should cause different price reactions from discretionary accounting changes made by the firm. He argues that discretionary accounting changes have the potential to act as a signal from the management about the economic welfare of the firm. Therefore, price reactions to discretionary changes should be greater than price reactions to mandated changes.

Watts and Zimmerman [1978] argue that price reactions should also be expected with mandated accounting changes. They note that effort and resources are used by businesses to influence mandated accounting decision by the FASB and SEC. They claim that accounting numbers are used in a number of ways that could influence the value of the firm. For example, taxes are based on accounting numbers and have cash flow implications. Also, management compensation contracts and bond covenant provisions often are based on accounting numbers. A change in accounting principles (either mandated or discretionary) could affect the status of those contracts.

Regulators and legislative bodies may also use accounting numbers to make decisions. The "windfall profits tax" was imposed on oil and gas firms in part because of high earnings numbers reported by these firms for several years.

To accommodate the potentially different effects of accounting changes, the following categories are used to analyze research in this section: (1) mandatory changes resulting in increased disclosure, (2) mandatory changes constraining accounting options for firms, and (3) discretionary accounting changes. Each of these types of accounting changes has different price implications and, therefore, requires different considerations in testing for market efficiency.

4.6.1 Mandatory Accounting Changes for Increased Disclosure

Many of the pronouncements of the SEC and FASB call for disclosure of information not previously reported. This information is usually available to the management and, possibly, to others through alternative information sources, but the regulatory action requires public disclosure in the 10-K or in the annual report. Given the shift from private information to public information, mandated increased disclosure offers an opportunity to test for strong-form market efficiency. Foster [1980], however, points out certain methodological problems in testing for the price effects of mandatory accounting changes. Because mandated accounting changes affect firms at the same time, there is a greater possibility of some other common information event affecting all the firms. This is an even greater problem when the mandatory accounting change affects only one industry. Therefore, all the tests of price effects of mandatory accounting changes are susceptible to the charge that some omitted variable is responsible for the results.

An early test of the effect of increased disclosure is due to Benston [1973]. He examines the change in riskiness and returns in stock prices surrounding the Securities Exchange Act of 1934. Prior to 1934 only 62 percent of the NYSE firms report sales. This group is used as a control group. The remaining NYSE firms are required to increase their disclosure with the Act of 1934. Benston observes no significant return or variance differences between the two groups before or after the requirement of increased disclosure. He argues that the Act of 1934 provides no new information of value to the market.

In more recent times, two requirements by the SEC have received a great deal of attention: line of business reporting and replacement cost reporting. The FASB has subsequently expanded on these disclosure requirements, but the initial regulatory action is due to the SEC. Each of these requirements substantially increased the information that is now in the public domain, although the information was probably available to management prior to the disclosure requirements.

With the advent of line of business reporting in 1970, the SEC also required restatement of accounting numbers by line of business for 1967–1969. This information, however, is not in annual reports prior to 1970. Collins [1975] addresses the question of whether this 1967–1969 line of business data could be used by an insider to make abnormal returns. He finds that such trading rules exist using business segment earnings forecasts. This suggests that the security prices did not fully reflect this information and is strong-form inefficient in regard to line of business reporting.

Horwitz and Kolodny [1977] examine security returns surrounding the month of the disclosure requirement for reporting lines of business. They compare the returns for firms that make line of business disclosures with those firms that do not make line of business disclosures. They discover no differences in returns, but their results are limited by the quality of the control group that may have had different characteristics than the experimental group.

Beaver, Christie, and Griffin [1980], Gheyara and Boatsman [1980], and Ro [1980] examine the return effects of the disclosure of replacement costs. All these studies find no significant relationship between prices and replacement costs. Watts and Zimmerman [1980] summarize the results of these three articles. The lack of results could be caused by the replacement cost data being already impounded in the price, which, in turn, implies that the market is strong-form efficient. There is also the possibility that the replacement cost data are irrelevant in valuing the security or that the methodology used is not sufficiently powerful to detect any return effects.

Noreen and Sepe [1981] examine returns surrounding the FASB's deliberations on whether inflation accounting should be required. They employ a "price reversal" method that can be used whenever a previous disclosure requirement is reversed. This method does not require the researcher to prespecify the direction of the price affect. Noreen and Sepe examine returns during (1) January 1974, when inflation disclosure was placed on the FASB agenda; (2) November 1975, when the FASB decided not to issue a statement on inflation accounting; and (3) January 1979, when the FASB once again proposed inflation accounting. They observe that positive abnormal returns during January 1974 are followed by negative abnormal returns during November 1975 and positive abnormal returns during January 1979. A similar reversing pattern is observed when negative abnormal returns occurred during January 1974. The problem with this method is that no insights are obtained on what is causing prices to change and, therefore, the study offers little information about market efficiency.

4.6.2 Mandatory Changes Constraining Accounting Principle Choice

There have been several recent cases of the FASB constraining the options that firms have in making accounting principle choices. By constraining accounting principle choice, the FASB hopes to improve cross-sectional comparability of financial results. The process of mandating certain accounting principles, however, causes firms using alternative accounting methods to make an accounting principle change to the acceptable method. On the surface, these accounting changes appear to have no direct economic effect on the firm. If so, market efficiency would dictate that no price reaction should accompany these accounting changes. Watts and Zimmerman [1978], however, pointed out that accounting numbers may be used for regulation and contracts, so a price effect may accompany a mandated accounting principle change.

FASB Statement No. 2, which related to research and development expenditures, provides one example of constraining an accounting option. Through this statement the FASB no longer allowed the capitalization of research and development expenditures. After 1974, firms were required to expense research and development costs immediately and to write off previously capitalized costs. Therefore, FASB No. 2 would tend to produce lower income figures if the firm previously capitalized research and development costs. Speculation that FASB No. 2 would reduce research and development expenditures was tested by Dukes, Dyckman, and Elliott [1980] and Horwitz and Kolodny [1980, 1981]. The results were mixed, but there is some indication that managers are concerned about the lower earnings caused by expensing research and development costs. Vigeland [1981], however, found no price reaction for those firms changing from capitalizing to expensing research and development costs. In a more recent study that tries to explain the different results, Elliott, Richardson, Dyckman, and Dukes [1984] suggest that the observed effect may have been due to economic events in the economy rather than to FASB No. 2.

Another accounting issue receiving considerable attention is accounting for foreign exchange. FASB No. 8 dichotomizes balance sheet items into groups that are closely associated with the monetary-nonmonetary classification scheme. Monetary items are converted at the current exchange rate while nonmonetary items are converted at the historical rate. Although this method caused considerable controversy in the business world, Dukes [1978] demonstrates that the returns of multinational firms are not affected by the issuance of FASB No. 8. In spite of this study, the FASB, responding in part to criticism of the statement, issued FASB No. 52, which called for the translation of all balance sheet items at the current exchange rate, and allowed the gain or loss to be reflected in retained earnings. At the time this is written, no studies have been completed on the price effects of FASB No. 52.

Pressure was also exerted on the FASB when it issued FASB Statement No. 19 on accounting for oil and gas companies. FASB No. 19 initially required the use of successful efforts in accounting for well drilling. Successful efforts require the immediate expensing of all costs incurred in drilling a dry well and, therefore, creates lower earnings than does the full-cost method, which allowed for capitalization of these costs. Dyckman and Smith [1979], Collins and Dent [1979], Lev [1979], and Larcker and Revsine [1983] conducted tests to see if the issuance of the exposure draft of FASB No. 19 had an adverse effect on the returns of those firms using the full-cost method. Although the results were mixed, there was evidence of a market reaction. Moreover, when the SEC later allowed full costing to be used, Smith [1981] and Collins, Rozeff, and Salatka [1982] observed a reversal of prices using the methodology of Noreen and Sepe [1981]. These studies appear to indicate a price reaction to mandated accounting changes for the oil and gas industry, but the causes of the price change and the implications for market efficiency remain unclear.

4.6.3 Discretionary Accounting Changes

In spite of increased attempts by the FASB to restrict accounting principle choices, there are still some choices that are left to the firm. These discretionary changes must be acceptable to the auditor and, in cases that involve taxes, acceptable to the Internal Revenue Service (IRS). Although the accounting changes must be accompanied by a "qualified" auditor's report, a large number of accounting changes are still observed.

The reasons for discretionary accounting changes are not adequately identified, but Watts and Zimmerman [1978] provide some plausible reasons related to contracts and regulations. Studies by Holthausen [1981], Leftwich [1981], Bowen, Lacey, and Noreen [1981], and others attempt to explain accounting principle choice with variables that may be related to contracts or regulation. The results are mixed. Discussions with managers indicate that they are concerned about direct price effects when accounting changes affect earnings. If accounting changes alone have a direct effect on prices, then the EMH could be rejected. The difficulty is in separating the price effects caused by investors being fooled by an accounting change from the price effects caused by either the accounting change influencing contracts and regulation or by any economic events that may have led to the accounting change.

One area of discretionary accounting choice is depreciation. Firms may choose from among several methods. Archibald [1972] investigates returns surrounding the accounting change from an accelerated method to a straight-line method. He observes that these firms have unusually low returns prior to the change, but no abnormal returns are obtained following the change.

The choice of accounting for acquisitions was discretionary before 1970, when APB No. 16 constrained that choice. Hong, Kaplan, and Mandelker [1978] investigate the return effects of choosing the purchase versus pooling-of-interests method prior to 1970. They find no evidence that the pooling-of-interest method, which is the more liberal accounting method, raised the stock prices of the acquiring firm.

Another area of discretionary accounting principle choice is inventory costing. With inflation, the first-in, first-out (FIFO) method generally results in higher earnings than does the last-in, last-out (LIFO) method. That fact makes the LIFO method attractive for tax purposes because fewer taxes must be paid on a lower income. But the IRS requires that firms use LIFO for financial reporting purposes if LIFO is used for tax purposes. Therefore, inventory costing change effects on prices are confounded by the tax effects.

Sunder [1973, 1975] observes no price changes surrounding changes to and from LIFO. He does observe some change in risk, however. In a later study, Ricks [1982] examines changes to LIFO in 1974. In this study, Ricks observes a decrease in prices following a change to LIFO. Prices, however, recovered within 12 months. This result is inconsistent with semistrong-form market efficiency and cannot be explained by tax, contract, or regulation effects. Those last effects should take place on the change date. If one assumes that the market is efficient and the abnormal returns are caused by a misspecified pricing model, then this study would indicate that the firms that changed to LIFO were inherently different from the control group.

4.7 SUMMARY

Even though accounting information is widely disseminated, there is a question of whether market prices adjust efficiently to earnings announcements. In particular, returns are larger than expected following the announcement of a large increase in earnings and smaller than expected following the announcement of a large decrease in earnings. These results are consistent with the papers demonstrating high returns for low-P/E stocks and low returns for high-P/E stocks. These abnormal returns occur gradually over time periods up to one year in length. While such results are consistent with market inefficiency, another explanation is that the pricing model is misspecified. This possibility is discussed further in the next chapter.

Changes or differences in accounting methods are a difficult medium for the study of market efficiency. Because management behavior may be affected by an accounting change through management's compensation package, a market reaction to an accounting change does not necessarily imply that the market is inefficient. Price reactions to accounting changes could also occur because accounting numbers are used in debt covenants and by regulators. Therefore, it is difficult to differentiate market reactions to accounting changes caused by real economic effects from those caused by investors being fooled by an accounting change.

CHAPTER FIVE

Market Inefficiency Results and the Adequacy of Pricing Models

A prominent theme in this book is the importance of the pricing model in testing for market efficiency. Any test of market efficiency also becomes a joint test of the pricing model. Most of the tests of market efficiency are based on empirical derivatives of the *capital asset pricing model* (CAPM). The original theoretical derivation of the CAPM, however, is based on several very restrictive assumptions. Considerable research has examined the effects of relaxing these assumptions. The first section of this chapter is a review of these papers.

Early empirical tests of the CAPM attempt to determine if returns coincide with their theoretical values. These tests are moderately successful, but later studies questioned their validity. The second section elaborates on these tests.

Dissatisfaction with the CAPM led to the search for an alternative model. The third section examines empirical tests of one result, the arbitrage pricing model.

The fourth section uses the results reviewed in the previous chapters to make inferences about the nature of the appropriate pricing model. If market efficiency is assumed, then consistent abnormal returns for certain firms following particular information events indicates an inappropriate pricing model. The empirical results are then used to help characterize the missing variables in the pricing model. Using a completely specified pricing model, there would be no abnormal returns.

5.1 RELAXING THE ASSUMPTIONS OF THE CAPM

The original derivation of the CAPM by Sharpe [1964] and Lintner [1965] is based on several very stringent assumptions. A riskless security is assumed to be available for borrowing and lending. Returns to holders of risky securities are assumed to be normally distributed. Investors are assumed to be risk averse, have homogeneous beliefs, and possess the same investment time horizon. Also, trading occurs with zero transaction costs. The stringency of these assumptions leads to the relative simplicity of the CAPM.

Later research attempts to relax the original assumptions to determine if the simplicity of the CAPM can be maintained. Some assumptions are found not to be critical. Other assumptions are found to be necessary and cannot be relaxed without severely affecting the validity of the CAPM. This section reviews the assumptions underlying the CAPM and discusses what happens when the assumptions are relaxed.

5.1.1 Existence of a Risk-Free Asset

One of the assumptions of the CAPM is that investors can borrow and lend at the same risk-free rate. This is not typically true for most investors. Investors are able to loan money to the U.S. government through the purchase of Treasury bills. These bills are probably the closest to being risk free of any security. But investors are usually not able to borrow money at the same interest rate as Treasury bills. Investors must pay a higher interest rate because they are perceived to be a more risky investment. Investors can become bankrupt.

Brennan [1971] addresses the problem of divergent borrowing and lending rates. He demonstrates that a pricing model that allows borrowing and lending rates to differ is very similar to the CAPM. In particular, the expected return of a security is still a linear function of the covariance of the returns of the security and the market portfolio of all assets. The linearity of the relationship between security returns and the return on the market portfolio is an important ingredient of many of the tests of the CAPM.

Black [1972] relaxes the assumption of borrowing and lending at the risk-free rate even further by not allowing a risk-free asset to exist. Instead, he replaces the risk-free asset with a portfolio that has a zero covariance with the market portfolio. Linear combinations of the zero-covariance (or zero-beta, as it is called) portfolio and the market portfolio completely describe the efficient frontier of mean-variance portfolio opportunities.

The existence of a risk-free asset is not critical to the CAPM. Although replacing the risk-free return with the return of a zero-covariance portfolio causes a slightly different testing procedure, the adjustments are relatively easy and the effects are minor.

5.1.2 Normality of the Distribution of Returns

The assumption of normally distributed returns simplifies the derivation of the CAPM. The normal return distribution can be described by two sets of parameters: the mean and the variance. Thus, a set of security returns are described by a *vector of means*, one for each security, and a *variance-covariance matrix* describing the interaction of the returns of the securities. The vector of means and the variance-covariance matrix are sufficient to describe completely the joint distribution of returns.

The assumption of normality also leads to the *separation theorem*. This theorem states that all investors are willing to hold linear combinations of only two portfolios if the joint returns' distribution is normal. These two portfolios are the market portfolio and the riskless asset, if it exists, or the zero covariance portfolio.

If security returns are more accurately described by distributions that require three moments (mean, variance, and skewness), the portfolio decisions and, therefore, the pricing of securities change. The normal distribution is no longer appropriate in this case since it is characterized by only two moments. Kraus and Litzenberger [1976] demonstrate that the additional moment causes another term in the pricing model. This term is related to the coskewness of the individual security return with the market portfolio return. A fourth moment would add yet another term, and so on.

An alternative to examining the effect of the return distribution on the CAPM is to look at the effect of risk preferences. For example, if every investor has a quadratic utility function, then the CAPM would hold for any distribution of returns as long as the variance is finite. The assumption of some other utility function requires a different form for the pricing model if no restrictions are placed on the return distributions.

5.1.3 Risk-Seeking Behavior

The CAPM is based on *risk-averse behavior* by investors. An investor is risk averse when willing to gamble only on an uncertain prospect with a positive expected return. A risk-seeking individual, on the other hand, would be willing to pay for a chance to engage in a bet with a negative expected return. With a little imagination, another individual could eventually lead the risk-seeking individual to ruin by offering multiple bets with negative expected returns. Therefore, persistent risk-seeking behavior is unlikely to exist for a long period of time. The assumption of risk averseness is critical to the CAPM and other derivative models based on portfolio theory. Without risk averseness, there would be no reason to diversify, and the covariance of the security returns with the return of the market portfolio would be irrelevant.

5.1.4 Heterogeneous Beliefs

The homogeneous belief assumptions of the CAPM is not an accurate characterization of the real world. With homogeneous beliefs, investors would hold combinations of the market portfolio and the riskless asset or the zero-covariance portfolio and trade only because of changes in wealth and consumption opportunities. Yet investors holding nondiversified portfolios and trading on information events such as earnings announcements are observed.

The homogeneous belief assumption, however, is not critical to the derivation of the CAPM. The CAPM formulation contains expectations of future returns for individual securities and the market portfolio. With homogeneous beliefs, these expectations are held by all investors. With heterogeneous beliefs, the expectations are weighted averages of individual expectations. These weights are a function of each individual's wealth and risk preferences. Lintner [1969] and Williams [1977] provide some examples of aggregating diverse beliefs into a pricing model.

There are, nevertheless, several problems with assuming heterogeneous beliefs for a pricing model. Unless further restrictions are placed on risk preferences or return distributions, the problem of aggregating diverse beliefs to obtain a consensus expectation for a pricing model becomes exceedingly difficult. Also, Ross [1978] points out that testing the CAPM is complicated using heterogeneous beliefs because empirical tests generally assume that the expectations of the CAPM are not systematically different from observable returns. The link between heterogeneous expectations and observable returns, however, is unclear.

5.1.5 Different Time Horizons

The original formulation of the CAPM is based on a single-period model. Investors are assumed to make portfolio decisions to maximize the expected utility of wealth at the end of the period. The world, however, is characterized by multiple periods of trading. Investors may attempt to maximize their expected utility over different time periods. Efforts exist to modify the CAPM to allow markets to reopen at discrete time periods or to allow trading to take place continuously. As in the case of relaxing other assumptions, more restrictive assumptions about risk preferences or return distributions are necessary to obtain pricing models similar to the CAPM.

A multiperiod model of the CAPM using discrete time periods is derived by Kraus and Litzenberger [1975]. To establish a pricing model similar to the CAPM, however, they assume that all investors have logarithmic utility functions that are independent of time and the state of the environment. With this assumption, investors make myopic investment decisions. Portfolios are formed through a series of one-period decisions.

Merton [1973] extends the CAPM to continuous time. He assumes that prices follow a Wiener or Brownian motion process. This process can be thought of as the continuous form of the one-period normally distributed return assumption of the CAPM. When interest rates are held constant, Merton is able to derive the continuous time version of the CAPM. If interest rates change, then the pricing model must incorporate this expected change in the investment opportunity set. In fact, additional variables must be added for each dimension of the investment opportunity set that changes. Changing interest rates complicates the extension of the CAPM into a multiperiod model.

Breeden [1979] attempts to simplify Merton's model by examining prices in terms of consumption rather than expected returns. He is able to descirbe a *pricing model with a single variable, aggregate real consumption*, rather than requiring variables for every dimension of the investment opportunity set that changes. Cornell [1981] notes that the changing investment opportunity set causes the coefficient on the aggregate real consumption to be nonstationary. Hence, the variables describing the investment opportunity set must be identified before empirical tests can be attempted.

The difficulty of adapting the CAPM to multiple periods is a problem. More theoretical and empirical research is necessary to describe adequately the adaptations necessary before the CAPM conforms to a multiperiod world.

5.1.6 Transaction Costs

One of the original assumptions of the CAPM is that investors can costlessly buy and sell securities. Under the assumptions of the CAPM, investors trade from their endowed portfolio position to some combination of the market portfolio and the riskless asset. Introducing transactions costs, such as brokerage fees, makes investors less willing to forsake their endowed portfolio position even though that position may not be diversified. Several articles examine the pricing effects if transaction costs prevent investors from being fully diversified.

Mayers [1973] considers the case when certain assets are not marketable. For example, an individual's future earning potential is not readily marketable. In this case, certain assets have infinite transaction costs. Under these circumstances, individual investors choose marketable securities that help them to diversify their nonmarketable assets. Given individual holdings of different nonmarketable assets, the market portfolio no longer is the optimal portfolio to hold.

Levy [1978] examines the pricing of securities when investors are limited to choosing only a certain number of securities. He suggests that transaction costs may limit the number of securities an investor is willing to hold. By holding a limited number of securities, investors are no longer completely diversified. When investors are completely diversified, the residual variance from the market model is an insignificant proportion of the risk borne by the investors and, therefore, should have no effect on prices. But when investors are not completely diversified, residual variance becomes proportionally greater and becomes part of the pricing mechanism. Mayshar [1981] also demonstrates this result by explicitly introducing transaction costs into portfolio choice decisions.

There are other transaction costs besides brokerage fees. For example, consider the limitations on selling securities short. A security is sold short by borrowing the security and then selling it. The security must eventually be purchased by the borrower and returned to the lender. Selling short is normally done when an investor believes that the price of a security will fall. The limitation on selling short is that the borrower of the security cannot receive the proceeds of selling the security. The proceeds are placed in escrow until the short position is eliminated. This makes selling short less attractive.

Miller [1977] examines pricing when selling short is not allowed and investors have heterogeneous beliefs. If no short selling is allowed, the most optimistic investors determine prices because the pessimistic investors are not able to sell the security short. This increases the supply of the security and decreases the price. Miller [1977] argues that constraining short sales for individual securities increases prices, but Jarrow (1980) demonstrates that the introduction of restrictions on short sales could either increase or decrease prices when considering a general equilibrium.

5.2 TESTING THE CAPITAL ASSET PRICING MODEL

Although the assumptions of the CAPM are very restrictive, the model may still provide a good description of the pricing of securities. The final test of a pricing model is its ability to predict future prices. There is, however, a special problem in testing the CAPM. The CAPM is based on expectations of returns, and these expectations are not directly observable.

Tests of the CAPM have commonly used past returns to proxy for future expected returns. To the extent that a correct assessment of future returns is made by investors, past returns provide a sampling of the distribution of expectations of future returns. Given that past returns are only a sampling of expected returns, however, large samples are necessary to accurately reflect expectations, and underlying causal conditions must remain essentially the same.

Even if past returns are a good surrogate for expected returns, the market return is still not easily observable. In earlier tests of the CAPM, some index of securities is commonly used to represent the market. Roll [1977], however, pointed out that the ability to observe the true market return, which should include the returns on all assets, is critical to testing the CAPM. He stated that the only direct test of the CAPM is a test of the mean-variance efficiency of the market portfolio. The CAPM can be refuted only if it can be demonstrated that the market portfolio is not mean-variance efficient. (Mean-variance efficiency occurs when no higher portfolio return can be attained for a given portfolio variance.) Roll's proofs cast serious doubts on the earlier tests of the CAPM. Nevertheless, these tests are reviewed in the following section to provide an historic perspective of tests of the CAPM.

5.2.1 Early Attempts to Test the CAPM

The early tests of the CAPM focus on three aspects of the return structure of securities:

1. The measurement of portfolio performance for securities with different betas
2. The linearity between beta and security returns
3. The effect of unsystematic risk on returns

These tests, while not direct tests of the CAPM, do offer empirical evidence that leads to reformulations of the model.

Friend and Blume [1970] notice that portfolios with high betas tend to perform poorly relative to portfolios with low betas. These results are obtained using market-adjusted individual security returns. The Treasury bill rate is used as a proxy for the risk-free rate. These ex post, individual security returns along with an estimated beta are then inserted into the CAPM to demonstrate the superior performance of the low-beta securities. Friend and Blume suggest several explanations for their results, including a bias in their estimates of betas and the inability to lend and borrow at the risk-free rate, but they do not test these hypotheses.

Black, Jensen, and Scholes [1972] use an instrumental variable approach to reduce the bias in estimating betas. Even with this approach, however, they find that high-beta securities do not perform as well as low-beta securities. They explain their results through the zero-beta portfolio model, which is the extension of the CAPM when no riskless asset exists. A zero-beta portfolio model still requires a linear relationship between beta and portfolio returns with the slope equal to the market return, but the intercept term is not constrained. Black, Jensen, and Scholes demonstrate that such a linear relationship has existed over 35 years. Roll [1977] points out, however, that this linear relationship only implies that the factors used by Black, Jensen, and Scholes are mean-variance efficient. A linear relationship will occur whenever betas are calculated against a mean-variance portfolio.

The linear relationship between beta and security returns is also tested by Fama and MacBeth [1973]. They test for linearity by adding a term to the linear model involving the square of beta. They determine that a linear relationship exists between beta and security returns by noting that the coefficient on the term involving the square of beta is not significantly different from zero. But, once again, the linear relationship occurs automatically when using a mean-variance portfolio to estimate betas.

Another attempt to test the CAPM receiving considerable attention involves the importance of unsystematic risk (residual variance) in explaining returns. Portfolio theory suggests that any risk that can be removed through diversification should not be rewarded. Hence, the CAPM should relate returns only to nondiversifiable risk, which is represented by beta.

An early study of the ability of the residual variance (unsystematic risk) to explain returns is due to Douglas [1969]. He finds a positive relationship between residual variance and returns, which is inconsistent with the CAPM. Subsequent studies, however, yield mixed results.

The most comprehensive study of the relationship between residual variance and returns is one by Miller and Scholes [1972]. They look at many different econometric issues that may affect the relationship. Attempts to explain the positive relationship due to misspecification errors are unsuccessful. After including the riskless rate, examining the linearity of the beta-return relationship and adjusting for heteroscedasticity, they still observe a positive relationship between the residual variance and returns. Miller and Scholes conclude that the relationship must be caused by errors in the variables used to represent the returns and risk. These errors could include measurement errors in estimating beta, lack of independence between sample moments caused by skewness, and use of an inappropriate market index. Roll [1977] shows that the use of an inappropriate market index is critical in testing the CAPM.

Other studies also investigate the effect of residual variance on returns. Fama and MacBeth [1973] note no significant relationship, while Levy [1978] finds a positive relationship. Friend, Westerfield, and Granito [1978] attempt to overcome the transition from an ex ante model to ex post returns by using expected returns based on earnings growth expectations published by financial institutions. The use of expected returns instead of ex post returns, however, still yields a positive relationship between residual variance and returns. Yet another paper by Foster [1978] finds no significant relationship between residual variance and returns after controlling for different levels of beta.

These early attempts reflect considerable differences of opinion concerning just how the CAPM should be tested. A number of econometric problems are present that lead to diverse empirical results and increase the uncertainty in the model. The paper by Roll [1977], referred to previously, helped to clarify some of the more critical issues involved in testing the CAPM. Roll's paper is discussed in more detail in the next section.

5.2.2 Efficiency of the Market Portfolio

Sharpe's [1964] CAPM is based on the assumption that security returns are jointly normal. He then demonstrates how the mean-variance frontier can be extended by assuming the existence of a riskless asset and a portfolio on the mean-variance frontier. Sharpe assumes that this combination is the market portfolio because all securities must be held in equilibrium. The pricing of securities is then determined by the covariance between the market portfolio and the individual security.

Roll (1977) shows that the critical issue in testing the CAPM is the mean-variance efficiency of the market portfolio. If the market portfolio is mean-variance efficient, then a linear relationship exists between the estimated beta and returns. The only empirical question that must be addressed in testing the CAPM is the mean-variance efficiency of the market portfolio. The validity of all the hypotheses tested in the previous section follows directly from the efficiency of the market portfolio, but, according to Roll, they cannot be independently tested.

Testing the mean-variance efficiency of the market portfolio, however, is not an easy task. The composition of the market portfolio is difficult if not impossible to determine. Most studies use some stock composite such as the S&P 500 to represent the market portfolio. But the market portfolio should include all assets. There are other types of assets in the world besides securities, of which many have returns that are, at best, difficult to observe.

The use of a proxy for the market portfolio can cause misleading results. If the proxy is mean-variance efficient, then a linear relationship between the estimated beta and returns exists, even though the true market portfolio is not mean-variance efficient. If the proxy is not mean-variance efficient, then a linear relationship does not exist, but nothing can be said about the mean-variance efficiency of the true market portfolio.

The existence of these problems in testing the CAPM has generally been acknowledged, although some researchers have questioned the severity of the problem. Blume [1980] looks at the relative mean-variance efficiency of bond portfolios, stock portfolios, and combinations of the two. The bond portfolio appears to be somewhat less efficient, but there is no clear dominance. Blume is careful to point out that determining the most efficient portfolio does not necessarily mean that it is the market portfolio. Stambaugh [1982] compares different market portfolios based on the linearity of the relationship of beta and returns. His portfolios involve various combinations of different assets, including stocks, bonds, Treasury bills, real estate, and personal assets. Linearity is not sensitive to composite indices with various proportions of the different types of assets. Stambaugh's results suggest that all these portfolios are on the mean-variance efficient frontier, but he says nothing about the efficiency of the market portfolio.

One of the most disturbing aspects of Roll's [1977] analysis is the inability to use the CAPM to measure portfolio performance. If deviations from the theoretical returns are observed, then either the market portfolio is not correctly specified or the CAPM is not an appropriate pricing model. If the CAPM is the appropriate model and the market portfolio can be determined, then no abnormal performance will be observed. These results imply that if the CAPM is valid, then the market is efficient because there will be no abnormal returns. Using the CAPM to test for market efficiency would, then, not be appropriate because assuming the CAPM implies market efficiency.

Mayers and Rice [1979] attempt to circumvent this problem by assuming the existence of an individual with superior information. All other individuals are assumed to have homogeneous beliefs and determine prices according to the CAPM. Mayers and Rice find that the individual with superior information, who has no effect on the price, earns an abnormal return based on the CAPM established by the other investors. Mayers and Rice interpret these results as a reinforcement of the use of the CAPM to determine abnormal returns. This paper also highlights the problem of testing the CAPM with the existence of heterogeneous beliefs. The question of whose beliefs are represented by the price formed by the CAPM could be unresolvable.

One method of evaluating portfolio performance that does not require an assumption of a specific pricing model has been suggested by Cornell [1979]. Under this method the return from a previous period, which incorporates risk premiums, is used as a base for comparison. This method is extremely simple, but, as Cornell points out, it is not a very powerful method statistically, because it does not control for changes in factors such as the return on the market. Also, there is an implicit assumption that the risk characteristics of securities do not change in a systematic manner with the experimental design. In other words, this method is not appropriate for testing a trading strategy based on a change in the debt-equity ratio because this ratio is likely to be tied to a change in risk. Using past returns as a benchmark, however, is an experimental method that should receive further consideration, especially with the uncertainty about the appropriate pricing models and whether certain pricing models such as the CAPM can be used to test for abnormal returns.

5.3 TESTING THE ARBITRAGE PRICING MODEL

The CAPM is the major theorectical model for explaining cross-sectional variability in asset returns. Roll's [1977] influential paper argues that, while testable in principle, the inability to observe the exact composition of the market portfolio specified by the theory makes an unambiguous test of the theory essentially impossible. Ross [1976, 1977] suggests the *arbitrage pricing model* (APM) as a testable alternative. The market portfolio does not play a critical part in the APM. Instead, asset returns are affected by the covariability of the asset's return with some set of random factors that influence the return.

Roll and Ross [1980] provide the first major attempt to test the APM. They initially attempt to determine the number of factors by performing factor analysis. Roll and Ross find that three to four factors seemed to underlie the return structure of individual securities. This process, however, is based on the past return series and does not necessarily provide the true factors. Roll and Ross recognized this problem and proposed a further test that would allow them to reject their estimated factor model. In tests of the capital asset pricing model, diversifiable risk is often identified as explaining return. Roll and Ross test the ability of diversifiable risk to explain returns in their arbitrage pricing model. A significant relationship would indicate that their model is misspecified because there should be no return to diversifiable risk. No significant relationship is found, which is consistent with their multifactor model. Unfortunately, it does not establish their multifactor model as the correct model of returns.

A similar test is performed by Reinganum [1981]. He estimates a multifactor model and then tests whether the small-firm effect is related to the residual. He discovers that the small-firm effect does not disappear with his multifactor model, which suggests that his model is misspecified.

Shanken [1982] and Jarrow [1983] argue that the arbitrage pricing model is not testable. Shanken points out that the factor model is influenced by the packaging of securities. He demonstrates that two equivalent sets of securities can lead to two different factor models. Jarrow [1983] indicates that part of arbitrage pricing theory is testable and part is not. The existence of arbitrage opportunities can be tested and, if found, would lead to the rejection of arbitrage pricing theory. Factor analysis can also be used to test for the existence of a finite number of orthogonal factors. But the expectational form of the model cannot be tested. With finite samples, the expectational relationship becomes only an approximation.

Testability of the APM can perhaps be achieved by placing more restrictions on the model. For example, Shanken [1982] suggests that a reasonable test of the arbitrage pricing model is to determine if the factors can explain all the variation in the return of the market portfolio. This procedure, however, would require the identification of the market portfolio, a problem that is critical in testing the capital asset pricing model. Shanken concludes, "factor analysis is merely concerned with statistical correlations and is blind to aggregate economic considerations. The failure of the usual empirical formulation of the APM to discriminate between alternative factor representations on the basis of such considerations is its fundamental weakness" [1982, p. 1137].

5.4 EMPIRICAL IMPLICATIONS ABOUT A FULLY SPECIFIED PRICING MODEL

Many of the studies discussed in the previous sections question the validity and testability of existing pricing models. Yet a pricing model is necessary (and sometimes sufficient) for testing market efficiency. This leaves the researcher interested in characterizing how information is used in securities markets with a difficult problem.

One method of circumventing the problem is to change the focus of the studies of market reactions to information. Instead of assuming a pricing model and testing for market efficiency, the researcher could assume market efficiency and investigate alternative pricing models. Many of the definitions discussed in Chapter 2 allow for market inefficiency only when information is not completely disseminated. When everyone has the information, markets are defined to be efficient. Therefore, the assumption that long-run returns are generated by an efficient market may be reasonable. Indeed, one would have to search for a theory to explain why markets would not be efficient in the long run.

By beginning with the assumption of market efficiency, experiments can be designed to generate and test pricing theories. One example of this approach is described in Section 3.2.6. Banz's [1981] results on the small-firm effect assumes that the abnormal returns are caused by a misspecification of the pricing model rather than by a market inefficiency. Subsequent studies on the small-firm effect attempt to explain the results by isolating the underlying factors affecting the abnormal returns. Although the testing process is continuing, a better understanding of the linkages among small firms, year-end tax effects, and P/E ratios now exists.

Simply identifying a market inefficiency does little to enhance our knowledge about information and securities markets. Further analysis is required to make inferences about how investors use the information to establish prices. Empirical results allow plausible hypotheses to be generated that can then be tested by alternative experimental methods using new data.

Suggesting that researchers assume market efficiency to test pricing models does not imply that market inefficiency be eliminated as a possible explanation for observed phenomena. But the responsibility of researchers is to search for rational explanations.

Only after alternative theories are exhaustively tested should market inefficiency be accepted as the explanation.

This discussion is based on studies that find long-term abnormal returns using the market model. As mentioned in Chapter 2, the pricing model is not as critical when examining returns that occur over a short period (e.g., within several days). Tests of the rapidity of price adjustments are both appropriate and valid in testing for market efficiency. These tests answer the question of how rapidly prices adjust to new information.

5.5 SUMMARY

In testing for market efficiency, the CAPM has often been assumed to describe the pricing process adequately. But the CAPM is based on very restrictive assumptions about investors and markets. Attempts to relax these assumptions generate alternative forms of the model. These models omit a risk-free asset (the zero-beta portfolio model), or add a preference for skewness, heterogeneous beliefs, different time horizons, and transaction costs.

Initial tests of the CAPM focus on the performance of portfolios with different betas, the linearity of beta and return, and the effect of nonsystematic risk on returns. Roll [1977], however, cautions that the underlying test of the CAPM is the mean-variance efficiency of the market portfolio. Unfortunately, the market portfolio is not easy to observe, which makes the testing of the CAPM difficult if not impossible.

Testing of the arbitrage pricing model has also met with limited success. A given set of data can always be represented by a finite number of factors. The problem is identifying those factors, specifying their economic significance, and relating them to expectations.

Given the uncertainty about the appropriate pricing model, tests of market efficiency remain difficult to interpret. An alternative approach is to assume market efficiency and use the empirical results to generate and test hypotheses about pricing models. This approach may provide a better understanding of how information is used in securities markets.

CHAPTER SIX

Implications for Accounting

The objective of this concluding chapter is to place the discussion of efficient markets as it relates to accounting in perspective. The following questions are addressed in this chapter:

1. Is the New York Stock Exchange efficient?
2. Of what importance and significance is efficiency to the market?
3. What implications does market efficiency have for accounting theory and practice?
4. What are the implications for accounting research?

6.1 IS THE NEW YORK STOCK EXCHANGE EFFICIENT?

The EMH is a statement about the functioning of organized markets for securities. The best known of these markets is the New York Stock Exchange (NYSE). Until recently, only data from the NYSE existed in adequate amounts and in a form readily accessible to researchers interested in empirical tests of the EMH. Hence, nearly all published research applies to the NYSE alone. Since few studies have been made of other markets, any conclusion about the efficiency of the NYSE can be extrapolated only with some chance of error to other organized markets. Firms listed on the NYSE are different from firms listed on other organized markets in several ways, including size and diversity of ownership. Firms listed on the NYSE are also more likely to be followed by financial analysts and the press. Therefore, if any market is efficient, the NYSE is the most likely candidate.

This book points out two major problems in attempting to answer the question of whether the NYSE is efficient: the first is deciding what market efficiency is; the second is determining how to test for market efficiency. Until these problems are resolved, conclusions about the efficiency of any market, including the NYSE, must be tentative.

The second chapter examines different definitions of market efficiency. Some definitions relate market efficiency to the proximity of expected prices to existing prices. The problem with this definition is the inability to observe expected prices. Other definitions of market efficiency are based on the distribution of information among investors. Prices are defined to be efficient with respect to a certain piece of information if they equal the prices that would exist if everyone has that information. This implies that markets can only be inefficient for private information. The problem in testing for market efficiency under this definition is in not being able to observe when information is received by all investors.

One of the purposes of carefully defining a concept such as market efficiency is to establish guidelines for testing purposes. The definitions presented in Chapter 2 do not provide much insight for testing market efficiency. The most common approach to investigating market efficiency is based on the fair-game concept. This concept states that a market is efficient if there is no trading strategy that yields a consistent abnormal return. There are two problems in using this method of testing for market efficiency: the first is that market efficiency cannot be "proved"; the second is in measuring abnormal returns.

There are an infinite number of possible trading strategies. To establish market efficiency under the fair-game concept, each of these trading strategies needs to be tested. This is an impossible task, so partial evidence must be relied on to make inferences about market efficiency. Like most theories in science, market efficiency may be rejected but it cannot be proved. Moreover, it is possible to reject market efficiency using a trading rule because of sampling error. The existence of a successful trading strategy over many years would be stronger grounds for rejecting market efficiency because sampling error is less likely to occur.

To test for market efficiency under the fair-game concept, a pricing model is needed to determine abnormal returns. Chapter 5 details some of the problems with the two most generally accepted pricing models: the CAPM and the arbitrage pricing model. Although derivative models of the CAPM are primarily used to test for market efficiency, there are questions about the validity and testability of the CAPM. Roll [1977] suggests that proving the CAPM is the same as proving market efficiency because no abnormal returns exist if the assumptions of the CAPM are valid. Testing of the arbitrage pricing model is also not particularly successful. Therefore, market efficiency is not a well defined concept, and its testable implications remain open to question.

Most "tests" of market efficiency examine trading strategies based on some information event. These tests assume that a risk factor (beta) estimated over a previous set of returns sufficiently described the pricing process. Any nonzero returns not explained by beta are considered a sign of market inefficiency. Using this testing process to answer the question of whether the NYSE is efficient, the answer is no. Substantial evidence indicates that firms with low P/E ratios experience higher than normal earnings increases, and firms with low capitalization tend to earn excessive returns over long time periods. This is particularly puzzling because these information items are readily observable. Why would the market be inefficient with respect to these information variables?

A more plausible explanation is that the pricing model used in these studies is misspecified. It is probable that an underlying omitted variable(s) in the pricing model is causing these firms to have higher returns. Since this variable(s) has not yet been identified, further research is necessary before an understanding of the pricing of securities is possible.

All empirical results that demonstrate market inefficiencies might be dismissed on the grounds of a misspecified pricing model, but normal returns from even a fully specified model are likely to approach zero for very short time periods. Therefore, any large changes in prices in the short run can be defined as abnormal returns. A case for market inefficiency can be made if prices are slow to adjust to new information. Several studies using intradaily return data indicate that abnormal returns following information announcements can exist for periods of up to several hours. These results suggest that the market is not perfectly efficient, yet only members of the exchange can profit from this information.

Although prices appear to adjust rapidly (although not instantaneously) to new information in an unbiased manner, the adjustment of prices to secondary information in the form of analysts' reports is troubling to those who believe in market efficiency. One possible explanation is that financial analysts are releasing new or private information concurrently with their reports.

The NYSE is probably inefficient with respect to private information. Although private information cannot be observed, insiders appear to earn abnormal returns on average. Also, there is evidence of large price movements caused by the release of information that is previously privately held.

From the evidence provided in this book a definitive conclusion on the efficiency of the NYSE cannot be drawn. There appear to be inefficiencies with respect to private information and for very short time periods following public announcements. The question of market efficiency with respect to public information is difficult if not impossible to resolve completely because of definitional and testing problems.

6.2 OF WHAT IMPORTANCE AND SIGNIFICANCE IS EFFICIENCY TO THE MARKET?

In the first place, an efficient market is a desirable state of affairs for society. To the extent that the market is efficient, securities are appropriately priced relative to one another based on publicly available information. The allocation of scarce resources among activities in such a market situation should be more nearly optimal than when no such relationship exists among security prices. Furthermore, no group of individual investors is placed at a disadvantage in such a market. To the extent that prices reflect all available information virtually instantaneously, individuals need not concern themselves with the search for over- and undervalued stocks, unless, of course, they possess information no one else has.

The EMH gives only a general statement of equilibrium return behavior. The market is constantly moving from one approximate equilibrium to another. In so doing, there will always be at least brief inefficiencies in the market. Indeed, it is in part a belief in the existence of these inefficiencies and the net benefit available from their discovery that hastens the adjustment process. If everyone were to believe in the instantaneous theory of adjustment, there would be no incentive to gather and use new information, which would, in turn, cause prices not to reflect information. Thus, the belief in at least some degree of inefficiency when new information becomes available is necessary to retain efficiency in the market. The implications have not been lost on specialists and brokers who are continually searching for such inefficiences. The activities of these individuals and the perspicacity with which they find new and better ways to perform their tasks affect the efficiency of the market.

Security prices and price changes affect the distribution of wealth and the related overall well-being of individuals. Since the total information system creates the forces leading to an equilibrium set of prices, it is entirely possible, as researchers in this area have indicated [Beaver, 1972], that alternate information systems could lead to different sets of market-clearing prices. Means by which such alternate equilibria can be predicted and their total impact on society evaluated do not yet exist. If or when several information systems lead to essentially the same market-clearing prices, then a choice among them can be based on an assessment of the cost of the system, including the costs of data collection, processing, storage, retrieval, and dissemination, as well as the monopoly profits and transaction costs arising in the arbitrage process. However, to the extent that such costs fall differently across individuals, the cost evaluation process reflects the same social welfare issues as exist in estimating the benefits.

6.3 WHAT IMPLICATIONS DOES MARKET EFFICIENCY HAVE FOR ACCOUNTING THEORY AND PRACTICE?

Accounting is only one element in the total information system. It has no monopoly on supplying information to the market. If the data it supplies become redundant or too costly for investors to use, it can and will be replaced by alternate sources. Questions that researchers should ask about accounting information are, does it supply relevant information? And, if so, do alternative information systems yield the same information? If so, the least expensive means of providing the relevant information should be used. (In determining the least cost alternative, differences in individual investor processing costs should be counted.) The question of just where accounting data have an overall comparative advantage in supplying information to the market needs answering.

In an efficient market, investors and preparers should not be concerned with where information is reported. Information reported in footnotes and the financial statements of the annual report and information filed with the SEC will all be impounded in security prices. Preparers and, by implication, policymakers, should be more concerned with cost-effective methods of reporting the information.

In addition, when there is an easy way to convert from one accounting method to another and the costs of conversion are insignificant, there should be little concern with a choice between the methods. Market efficiency guarantees that all information contained in both measures will be promptly and properly reflected in the security price. If costs of conversion are significant, however, consideration should be given to reporting based on both methods if there is an insignificant cost of doing so.

More explicit attempts have been made to use the concept of market efficiency to make accounting principle choices. Beaver and Dukes [1973], for example, suggest using the accounting method most highly associated with security prices, subject to cost-benefit considerations. Their approach is based on the acceptance of efficiency in the market. If the market is efficient, then security prices reflect the available information. To facilitate the process, where two ways of reporting the same information exist, it is logical to report the information that seems to be impounded in prices, namely, that most consistent with the information set underlying security prices. In this way, the (efficient) market indirectly indicates the preferred reporting method.

A problem with this approach to choosing among alternative accounting methods is recognized by Beaver [1973] and Gonedes and Dopuch [1974]. Different individuals experience different effects in terms of how well off they are under these choices. Hence, to make a choice among accounting alternatives results in social effects that researchers do not yet know how to measure. This issue, which has been mentioned before, requires resolution before optimal choices can be made.

In addition, the research methodology employed is not adequate to support the conclusions suggested. May and Sundem [1973] point to an important limitation in the Beaver-Dukes approach. Consider a new accounting information system based on replacement cost that provides, as does the existing one based on historical cost, information not otherwise available to the market. Suppose, further, that there is some, but not complete, overlap in the information supplied by the two systems. The new system may benefit society to the extent that it reports new information not otherwise available. Yet it is possible that the association between security prices and measures supplied by the proposed system will be lower, since the potential new information is not presently available to the market.

Beaver and Demski [1974] assert that an association test cannot "in and of itself imply or dictate a preference for one reporting practice over another" [p. 10]. To make these judgments, the market price must reflect the value of the information production activities. Beaver [1974] puts it succinctly: "although evidence [in particular association tests between accounting data and security price behavior] cannot indicate what choice to make, it can provide information on the potential consequences of various choices. . . . The ultimate issue is the extent to which this simplified preference ordering [for accounting reporting alternatives] is consistent with the ordering obtained under a complete analysis" [p. 570].

Although the EMH cannot be used to make decisions on accounting methods other than to report both methods if increased disclosure is costless, accounting policymakers should be and are concerned about the effect of accounting principle choices on stock prices. Stock prices affect the welfare of individuals. The FASB has requested research on the impact of their announcements on stock prices. Recognition of the relationship between accounting information and stock prices by the Board is an important step in incorporating market research as a factor in making policy decisions.

To the extent the EMH can be accepted, accounting policy should strive to increase investor awareness of the fact that reported accounting data are not likely to be useful in detecting over- or under-valued securities. Searching for such securities simply leads to increased transaction costs, the likelihood of improper diversification, and the possibility of a portfolio with inappropriate risk characteristics.

The choice of the amount of information disclosure is affected by the potential market inefficiencies with respect to private information. If insiders are allowed to trade on private information, then there will be a net transfer of wealth from outside investors to inside investors. More immediate and complete disclosure could preempt the ability of insiders to earn abnormal returns. While the decision to increase disclosure is a policy decision that must be made with the appropriate social welfare trade-offs, tests of market efficiency have provided some information about the wealth transfers under the existing reporting system.

6.4 WHAT ARE THE IMPLICATIONS FOR ACCOUNTING RESEARCH?

Financial accounting research is generally concerned with how individuals use information in a market setting. Analytical research provides theories on how information should be used in markets. Empirical research attempts to describe how information is actually being used in markets. The joint results from this research can then ideally be used by policymaking bodies that regulate accounting choice.

Although significant progress has been made in financial

accounting research in the last 20 years, the EMH has often misled rather than guided accounting researchers. Significant effort has been applied to testing the EMH. But other than testing for the short-run (within several days) adjustment of prices, testing the EMH through the examination of market prices seems hopeless. Any indication of abnormal returns from a trading strategy can always be attributed to a misspecified pricing model.

The major research proposal of this book is to treat the EMH as a maintained hypothesis. By assuming that investors use information to determine demands for securities (and, thus, prices), the research focus can be placed on the more important issue of how investors use information and how that information affects their individual welfare.

Accounting researchers, unfortunately, cannot directly observe individual investor use of information. Public information releases can be observed as well as the market reaction to those public announcements. Inferences about investor use of information must be made from the association between information and market reactions.

Therefore, continued studies of the relationship between information and market reactions are of value if the results are to allow inferences about how individuals use information to be made. A better understanding of how individuals use information in a market setting not only leads to more informed accounting policy-makers, but also provides a basis for better pricing models. The use of securities market research to determine more appropriate pricing models is discussed in Chapter 5.

Researchers must not only be concerned with how investors use information, but also with how investor welfare is affected by information production. Once again, however, individual investor welfare cannot be observed. Rather, the researcher must rely on inferences from market reactions to information announcements.

Because researchers hope to draw many inferences from the relationship between information and market reactions, expanding the set of types of information events and market reactions to obtain a greater number of relationships could be useful. For example, there are many types of market reactions that researchers can observe such as price changes, trading volume, short selling, and others. Using multiple market reactions could expand our understanding of the effect of information in security markets.

Testing relationships between information announcements and market reactions that do not lead to inferences about the underlying use of the information, however, is a futile exercise. The design of empirical research should be carefully formulated so as to yield a better understanding of how information is being used. Although a complete understanding of the use of information by each individual investor is unlikely, researchers are capable of providing policymakers with some general effects of existing accounting policy and a general framework of how information is used in markets.

6.5 SUMMARY

The research in accounting spawned by the EMH, and supported by research in economics and in finance on portfolio theory and capital asset pricing, has made substantive contributions to both accounting research methodology and the logic of the issues investigated. It does a much needed task of tying empirical research to theory and showing the relevance of the issues addressed to a complete program of accounting research. Moreover, this research has, through its empirical findings, an important feedback effect on the theoretical developments of equilibrium pricing models as well as on the selection of research methodology. Yet this strand of analysis covers only a segment, albeit an important one, of the total economic activity to which even the accounting information system relates.

Recommendations for accounting policy should not be based solely on the findings of such research efforts. The theory is still developing, and the tests are no better than the theory on which the empirical work is based. Few if any results are free from limiting assumptions (theoretical and methodological), and some faith is required in generalizing or in being comfortable that the context to which a research result is applied is adequately specified. Moreover, even if the findings can be accepted, policy decisions involve moral judgments as well. The information desires of individuals remain even in an efficient market.

Given an efficient market, researchers and others can examine the consequences of various policy decisions. By looking at relationships between information and market reactions, inferences about investor uses of information are possible. These inferences, however, are subject to theories about the information usage in markets. Theory must become more global and testing more precise and complete before broad accounting policy solutions can stand adequately on the resulting foundation. Until that time, accountants will continue to find sufficient reasons to support different solutions to accounting problems. One's choice will hinge largely on one's prior beliefs in the adequacy of the underlying theory; the validity of the supportive research; the practical implication of the information system choice, including the impact on social welfare and economic activity; and the costs (political and other) of implementation.

Research in efficient markets is adding to the implements available to address these issues, but the researcher has not and will not solve all reporting problems. Proponents of the EMH and its implications often claim too much while its detractors give it too little. As with most innovations, the truth lies nearer the middle ground.

Bibliography

ABDEL-KHALIK, A., and B. AJINKYA, "Returns to Informational Advantages: The Case of Analysts' Forecast Revisions," *The Accounting Review* (October 1982), pp. 661–680.

AHARONY, J., and S. ITZHAK, "Quarterly Dividend and Earnings Announcements and Stockholders' Returns: Am Empirical Analysis," *Journal of Finance* (March 1980), pp. 1–12.

ALEXANDER, S., "Price Movements in Speculative Markets: Trends or Random Walks," *Industrial Management Review* (May 1961), pp. 7–26.

ALTMAN, E., "Financial Ratios, Discriminant Analysis and the Prediction of Corporate Bankruptcy," *Journal of Finance* (September 1968), pp. 589–609.

——, and M. BRENNER, "Information Effects and Stock Market Response to Signs of Firm Deterioration," *Journal of Finance and Quantitative Analysis* (March 1981), pp. 35–51.

ARBEL, A., and P. STREBEL, "Pay Attention to Neglected Firms," *Journal of Portfolio Management* (Winter 1983), pp. 37–42.

ARCHIBALD, T., "Stock Market Reaction to the Depreciation Switch-Back," *The Accounting Review* (January 1972), pp. 22–30.

ASQUITH, P., and E. KIM, "The Impact of Merger Bids on the Participating Firms' Security Holders," *Journal of Finance* (December 1982), pp. 1209–1228.

BACHELIER, L., "Théorie de la Spéculation" (Paris: Gauthier-

Villars, 1900), translated version in Paul Cootner, *The Random Character of Stock Market Prices*, pp. 17-28. Cambridge, Mass.: M.I.T. Press, 1964.

BALL, R., "Changes in Accounting Techniques and Stock Prices," *Journal of Accounting Research, Supplement* (1972), p. 1-37.

_____ , "Anomalies in Relationships Between Securities Yields and Yield Surrogates," *Journal of Financial Economics* (June/September 1978), pp. 103-126.

_____ , and P. BROWN, "An Empirical Evaluation of Accounting Income Numbers," *Journal of Accounting Research* (Autumn 1968), pp. 159-178.

BANZ, R., "The Relationship Between Return and Market Value of Common Stocks," *Journal of Financial Economics* (March 1981), pp. 3-18.

BASU, S., "The Investment Performance of Common Stocks in Relation to Their Price-Earnings Ratios: A Test of the Efficient Market Hypothesis," *Journal of Finance* (June 1977), pp. 663-682.

_____ , "The Effect of Earnings Yield on Assessments of the Association Between Annual Accounting Income Numbers and Security Prices," *The Accounting Review* (July 1978), pp. 599-625.

_____ , "The Relationship Between Earnings Yield, Market Value, and Return for NYSE Common Stocks: Further Evidence," *Journal of Financial Economics* (June 1983), pp. 129-156.

BEAVER, W., "The Information Content of Annual Earnings Announcements," *Journal of Accounting Research, Supplement* (1968), pp. 67-92.

_____ , "The Behavior of Security Prices and Its Implication for Accounting Research (Methods)," *Supplement to the Accounting Review* (1972), pp. 407-437.

_____ , "What Should Be the Objectives of the FASB?" *Journal of Accounting* (August 1973), pp. 49-56.

_____ , "Implications of Security Price Research for Accounting: A Reply to Bierman," *The Accounting Review* (July 1974), pp. 563-571.

_____ , "Market Efficiency," *The Accounting Review* (January 1981), pp. 23-37.

_____ , A. CHRISTIE, and P. GRIFFIN, "The Information Content of SEC ASR #190," *Journal of Accounting and Economics* (August 1980), pp. 127-158.

_____ , and J. DEMSKI, "The Nature of Financial Accounting Objectives," *Journal of Accounting Research, Supplement* (1974) pp. 170-182.

_____ , and R. DUKES, "Tax Allocation and δ-Depreciation Methods," *The Accounting Review* (July 1973), pp. 549-559.

_____ , T. KETTLER, and M. SCHOLES, "The Association Between Market Determined and Accounting Determined Risk Measures," *The Accounting Review* (October 1970), pp. 654-682.

_____ , and W. LANDSMAN, "Note on the Behavior of Residual Security Returns for Winner and Loser Portfolios," *Journal of Accounting and Economics* (December 1981), pp. 233-242.

_____ , and D. MORSE, "What Determines Price-Earnings Ratios?" *Financial Analysts Journal* (July-August 1978), pp. 65-76.

BENSTON, G., "Required Disclosure and the Stock Market: An Evaluation of the Securities Exchange Act of 1934," *American Economic Review* (March 1973), pp. 132-154.

BLACK, F., "Capital Market Equilibrium with Restricted Borrowing," *Journal of Business* (July 1972), pp. 444-455.

_____ , "Yes Virginia, There Is Hope: Test of the Value Line Ranking System," *Financial Analysts Journal* (September-October 1973).

_____ , M. JENSEN, and M. SCHOLES, "The Capital Asset Pricing Model and Some Empirical Tests." In M. Jensen, Ed., *Studies in the Theory of Capital Markets*. New York: Praeger, 1972, pp. 79-121.

_____ , and M. SCHOLES, "The Pricing of Options and Corporate Liabilities," *Journal of Political Economics* (May-June 1973), pp. 637-654.

BLUME, M., "The Relative Efficiency of Various Portfolios: Some Further Evidence," *Journal of Finance* (May 1980), pp. 269-283.

BONIN, J., and E. MOSES, "Seasonal Variations in Prices of Individual Dow-Jones Industrial Stocks," *Journal of Financial and Quantitative Analysis* (December 1974), pp. 963-991.

BOWEN, R., J. LACEY, and E. NOREEN, "Determinants of the Corporate Decision to Capitalize Interest," *Journal of Accounting and Economics* (August 1981), pp. 151-179.

BRADLEY, M., "Interfirm Tender Offers and the Market for Corporate Control," *Journal of Business* (October 1980), pp. 345-376.

BRANCH, B., "A Tax Loss Trading Rule," *Journal of Business* (April 1977), pp. 198-207.

BREEDEN, D., "An Intertemporal Asset Pricing Model with Stochastic Consumption and Investment Opportunities," *Journal of Financial Economics* (September 1979), pp. 265-296.

BRENNAN, M., "Capital Market Equilibrium with Divergent Borrowing and Lending Rates," *Journal of Financial and Quantitative Methods* (December 1971), pp. 1197-1206.

BRILOFF, A., *Unaccountable Accounting*. New York: Harper & Row, 1972.

_____ , "Dirty Pooling," *Barron's*, July 15, 1968.

_____ . "You Deserve a Break . . . . ," *Barron's*, July 8, 1974.

BROWN, P., D. KEIM, A. KLEIDON, and T. MARSH, "Stock Return Seasonalities and the Tax-Loss Selling Hypothesis: Analysis of the Arguments and Australian Evidence," *Journal of Financial Economics* (June 1983), pp. 105-128.

____ , and J. KENNELLY, "The Informational Content of Quarterly Earnings: An Extension and Some Further Evidence," *Journal of Business* (July 1972), pp. 403–415.

BROWN, S., "Earnings Changes, Stock Prices, and Market Efficiency," *Journal of Finance* (March 1978), pp. 17–28.

CAREY, K., "Nonrandom Price Changes in Association with Trading in Large Blocks: Evidence of Market Efficiency in Behavior of Investor Returns," *Journal of Business* (October 1977), pp. 407–414.

CHAREST, G., "Split Information, Stock Returns and Market Efficiency—I," *Journal of Financial Economics* (June/September 1978), pp. 265–296. (a)

____ , "Dividend Information, Stock Returns and Market Efficiency—II," *Journal of Financial Economics* (June/September 1978), pp. 297–330. (b)

COLLINS, D., "SEC Product-Line Reporting and Market Efficiency," *Journal of Financial Economics* (June 1975), pp. 125–164.

____ , and W. DENT, "The Proposed Elimination of Full Cost Accounting in the Extractive Petroleum Industry: An Empirical Assessment of the Market Consequences," *Journal of Accounting and Economics* (March 1979), pp. 3–44.

____ , M. ROZEFF, and W. SALATKA, "The SEC's Rejection of SFAS No. 19: Tests of Market Price Reversal," *The Accounting Review* (January 1982), pp. 1–17.

COMISKEY, E., "Market Response to Changes in Depreciation Accounting," *The Accounting Review* (April 1971), pp. 279–285.

COOPER, R., "Efficient Capital Markets and the Quantity Theory of Money," *Journal of Finance* (June 1974), pp. 887–908.

COPELAND, T., and D. MAYERS, "The Value Line Enigma (1965–1978): A Case Study of Performance Evaluation Issues," *Journal of Financial Economics* (November 1982), pp. 289–322.

CORNELL, B., "Asymmetric Information and Portfolio Performance Measurement," *Journal of Financial Economics* (December 1979), pp. 381–390.

____ , "The Consumption Based Asset Pricing Model: A Note on Potential Tests and Applications," *Journal of Financial Economics* (March 1981), pp. 103–108.

CROSS, F., "The Behavior of Stock Prices on Friday and Monday," *Financial Analysts Journal* (November/December 1973), pp. 67–69.

DANN, L., D. MAYERS, and R. RAAB, "Trading Rules, Large Blocks and the Speed of Price Adjustment," *Journal of Financial Economics* (1977), pp. 3–22.

DAVIES, P., and M. CANES, "Stock Prices and the Publication of Second-Hand Information," *Journal of Business* (January 1978), pp. 43–56.

DODD, P., "Merger Proposals, Management Discretion, and Stockholder Wealth," *Journal of Financial Economics* (June 1980), pp. 105–138.

_____ , and R. RUBACK, "Tender Offers and Stockholder Returns: An Empirical Analysis," *Journal of Financial Economics* (December 1977), pp. 351–373.

DOUGLAS, G., "Risk in the Equity Markets: An Empirical Appraisal of Market Efficiency," *Yale Economic Essays* (Spring 1969), pp. 3–45.

DUKES, R., *An Empirical Investigation of the Effects of Statement of Financial Accounting Standards No. 8 on Security Return Behavior*, FASB Research Report, Financial Accounting Standards Board, Stamford, Conn. 1978.

_____ , T. DYCKMAN, and J. ELLIOTT, "Accounting for Research and Development Costs: The Impact on Research and Development Expenditures," *Journal of Accounting Research, Supplement* (1980), pp. 1–37.

DYCKMAN, T., and A. SMITH, "Financial Accounting and Reporting by Oil and Gas Producing Companies: A Study of Information Effects," *Journal of Accounting and Economics* (March 1979), pp. 45–76.

DYL, E., "Capital Gains Taxation and Year-End Stock Market Behavior," *Journal of Finance* (March 1977), pp. 165–175.

EASLEY, D., and R. JARROW, "Consensus Beliefs Equilibrium and Market Efficiency," *Journal of Finance* (June 1982), pp. 903–912.

ELLIOTT, J., "'Subject to' Audit Opinions and Abnormal Security Returns: Outcomes and Ambiguities," *Journal of Accounting Research* (Autumn 1982), pp. 617–638.

_____ , G. RICHARDSON, T. DYCKMAN, and R. DUKES, "The Impact of SFAS #2 on Firm Expenditures in Research and Development," *Journal of Accounting Research* (Spring 1984), pp. 85–102.

ELTON, E., and M. GRUBER, "Marginal Stockholder Tax Rates and the Chentele Effect," *Review of Economics and Statistics* (February 1970), pp. 68–74.

FAMA, E., "The Behavior of Stock Market Prices," *Journal of Business* (January 1965), pp. 34–105.

_____ , "Efficient Capital Markets: A Review of Theory and Empirical Work," *Journal of Finance* (May 1970), pp. 383–417.

_____ , "Efficient Capital Markets: Reply," *Journal of Finance* (March 1976), pp. 143–154.

_____ , and M. BLUME, "Filter Rules and Stock Market Trading," *Journal of Business* (January 1966), pp. 226–241.

_____ , L. FISHER, M. JENSEN, and R. ROLL, "Tha Adjustment of Stock Prices to New Information," *International Economic Review* (February 1969), pp. 1–21.

_____ , and J. MACBETH, "Risk, Return, and Equilibrium: Empirical Tests," *Journal of Political Economics* (May/June 1973), pp. 607–636.

FIGLEWSKI, S., "Market 'Efficiency' in a Market with Heterogeneous Information," *Journal of Political Economics* (August 1978), pp. 581–597.

_____ , "The Informational Effects of Restriction on Short Sales: Some Empirical Evidence," *Journal of Financial and Quantitative Analysis* (November 1981), pp. 463–476.

FINNERTY, J., "Insiders and Market Efficiency," *Journal of Finance* (September 1976), pp. 1141–1148.

FIRTH, M., "Qualified Audit Reports: Their Impact on Investment Decisions," *The Accounting Review* (July 1978), pp. 642–650.

FORSYTHE, R., T. PALFREY, and C. PLOTT, "Asset Valuation in an Experimental Market," *Econometrica* (May 1982), pp. 537–567.

FOSTER, G., "Asset Pricing Models: Further Tests," *Journal of Financial and Quantitative Analysis* (March 1978), pp. 39–53.

_____ , "Briloff and the Capital Market," *Journal of Accounting Research* (Spring 1979), pp. 262–274.

_____ , "Accounting Policy Decisions and Capital Market Research," *Journal of Accounting and Economics* (March 1980), pp. 29–62.

_____ , C. OLSEN, and T. SHEVLIN, "Earnings Releases, Anomalies and the Behavior of Security Returns," *Accounting Review* (October 1984), pp. 574–603.

FOSTER, T., and D. VICKREY, "The Information Content of Stock Dividend Announcements," *The Accounting Review* (April 1978), pp. 360–370.

FRENCH, K., "Stock Returns and the Weekend Effect," *Journal of Financial Economics* (March 1980), pp. 55–69.

FRIEND, I., and M. BLUME, "Measurement of Portfolio Performance Under Uncertainty," *American Economic Review* (September 1970), pp. 561–575.

_____ , R. WESTERFIELD, and M. GRANITO, "New Evidence on the Capital Asset Pricing Model," *Journal of Finance* (June 1978), pp. 903–917.

GHEYARA, K., and J. BOATSMAN, "Market Reaction to the 1976 Replacement Cost Disclosures," *Journal of Accounting and Economics* (August 1980), pp. 107–126.

GIBBONS, M., and P. HESS, "Day of the Week Effects and Asset Returns," *Journal of Business* (October 1981), pp. 579–596.

GIVOLY, D., and T. LAKONISHOK, "The Information Content of Financial Analysts 'Forecasts of Earnings': Some Evidence on Semi-Strong Inefficiency," *Journal of Accounting and Economics* (December 1979), pp. 165–186.

_____ , and A. OVADIA, "Year-End Tax-Induced Sales and Stock Market Seasonality," *Journal of Finance* (March 1983), pp. 171–185.

GONEDES, N., "The Significance of Selected Accounting Procedures: A Statistical Test," *Journal of Accounting Research, Supplement* (1969), pp. 90–113.

_____ , and N. DOPUCH, "Capital Market Equilibrium, Information-Production and Selecting Accounting Techniques: Theoretical Framework and Review of Empirical Work," *Journal of Accounting Research, Supplement* (1974), pp. 48-169.

GRAHAM, B., *The Intelligent Investor*. New York: Harper & Row, 1973.

GRANGER, C., and O. MORGENSTEIN, "Spectral Analysis of New York Stock Market Prices," *Kyklos*, 16 (1963), pp. 1-27.

GRANT, E., "Market Implications of Differential Amounts of Interim Information," *Journal of Accounting Research* (Spring 1980), pp. 225-268.

GRIER, R., and R. ALBIN, "Non-Random Price Changes in Association with Trading in Large Blocks," *Journal of Business* (July 1973), pp. 425-435.

GROSSMAN, S., "On the Efficiency of Competitive Stock Prices When Traders Have Diverse Information," *Journal of Finance* (May 1976), pp. 573-585.

_____ , "An Introduction to the Theory of Rational Expectations Under Asymmetric Information," *Review of Economic Studies* (October 1981), pp. 541-559.

_____ , and J. STIGLITZ, "On the Impossibility of Informationally Efficient Markets," *American Economic Review* (June 1980), pp. 393-408.

HARRISON, T., "Different Market Reactions to Discretionary and Nondiscretionary Accounting Changes," *Journal of Accounting Research* (Spring 1977), pp. 84-107.

HESS, A. and P. FROST, "Tests for Price Effects of New Issues of Seasonal Securities," *Journal of Finance* (March 1982), pp. 11-26.

HOLTHAUSEN, R., "Evidence on the Effect of Bond Covenants and Management Compensation Contracts on the Choice of Accounting Technique," *Journal of Accounting and Economics* (March 1981), pp. 73-109.

HOMA, K., and D. JAFFEE, "The Supply of Money and Common Stock Prices," *Journal of Finance* (December 1971), pp. 1045-1066.

HONG, H., R. KAPLAN, and G. MANDELKER, "Pooling vs. Purchase: The Effects of Accounting for Mergers on Stock Prices," *The Accounting Review* (January 1978), pp. 31-47.

HOPEWELL, M., and A. SCHWARTZ, "Stock Price Movement Associated with Temporary Trading Suspensions: Bear Market vs. Bull Market," *Journal of Financial and Quantitative Analysis* (November 1976), pp. 577-590.

_____ , and A. SCHWARTZ, "Temporary Trading Suspensions in Individual NYSE Securities," *Journal of Finance* (December 1978), pp. 1355-1373.

HORWITZ, B., and R. KOLODNY, "Line of Business Reporting and Security Prices: An Analysis of an SEC Disclosure Rule, *Bell Journal of Economics* (Spring 1977), pp. 234-249.

_____ , and R. KOLODNY, "The Economic Effects of Involuntary Uniformity in the Financial Reporting of R&D Expenditures," *Journal of Accounting Research, Supplement* (1980), pp. 38-74.

_____ , and R. KOLODNY, "The FASB, the SEC, and R&D," *Bell* (Spring 1981), pp. 249-262.

IBBOTSON, R., "Price Performance of Common Stock New Issues," *Journal of Financial Economics* (September 1975), pp. 235-272.

JAFFE, J., "Special Information and Insider Trading," *Journal of Business* (July 1974), pp. 410-428. (a)

_____ , "The Effect of Regulation Changes on Insider Trading," *Bell Journal of Economics* (Spring 1974), pp. 93-121. (b)

JARROW, R., "Heterogeneous Expectation, Restrictions on Short Sales, and Equilibrium Asset Prices," *Journal of Finance* (December 1980), pp. 1105-1114.

_____ , "A Generalized Arbitrage Pricing Theory," Working Paper, Cornell University, Ithaca, New York, 1983.

JENSEN, M., "Random Walks: Reality and Myth—Comment," *Financial Analysts Journal* (November–December 1967), pp. 77-85.

_____ , "The Performance of Mutual Funds in the Period 1945-1964," *Journal of Finance* (May 1968), pp. 389-416.

_____ , and G. BENNINGTON, "Random Walks and Technical Theories; Some Additional Evidence," *Journal of Finance* (May 1970), pp. 469-482.

JONES, C., and R. LITZENBERGER, "Quarterly Earnings Reports and Intermediate Stock Price Trends," *Journal of Finance* (March 1970), pp. 143-148.

JOY, O., R. LITZENBERGER, and R. MCENALLY, "The Adjustment of Stock Prices to Announcements of Unanticipated Changes in Quarterly Earnings," *Journal of Accounting Research* (October 1977), pp. 207-225.

KEIM, D., "Size-Related Anomalies and Stock Return Seasonality: Further Empirical Evidence," *Journal of Financial Economics* (June 1983), pp. 13-32.

KEOWN, A., and J. PINKERTON, "Merger Announcements and Insider Trading Activity: An Empirical Investigation," *Journal of Finance* (September 1981), pp. 855-870.

KIGER, J., "An Empirical Investigation of NYSE Volume and Price Reactions to the Announcements of Quarterly Earnings," *Journal of Accounting Research* (Spring 1972), pp. 113-128.

KIHLSTROM, R., and L. MIRMAN, "Information and Market Equilibrium," *Bell Journal of Economics* (Spring 1975), pp. 357-376.

KLEIN, R., and V. BAWA, "The Effect of Limited Information and Estimation Risk on Optimal Portfolio Diversification," *Journal of Financial Economics* (August 1977), pp. 89-111.

KON, S., and F. JEN, "The Investment Performance of Mutual

Funds: An Empirical Investigation of Timing, Selectivity, and Market Efficiency," *Journal of Business* (April 1979), pp. 263-289.

KRAUS, A., and R. LITZENBERGER, "Market Equilibrium in a Multiperiod State Preference Model with Logarithmic Utility," *Journal of Finance* (December 1975), pp. 1213-1228

_____ , and R. LITZENBERGER, "Skewness Preference and the Valuation of Risk Assets," *Journal of Finance* (September 1976), pp. 1085-1100.

_____ , and H. STOLL, "Price Impacts of Block Trading on the NYSE," *Journal of Finance* (June 1972), pp. 569-588.

KRYZANOWSKI, L., "The Efficacy of Trading Suspensions: A Regulatory Action Designed to Prevent the Exploitation of Monopoly Information," *Journal of Finance* (December 1979), pp. 1187-1200.

LAKONISHOK, J., and M. LEVI, "Weekend Effects on Stock Returns: A Note," *Journal of Finance* (June 1982), pp. 883-889.

LARCKER, D., and P. REVSINE, "The Oil and Gas Accounting Controversy: An Analysis of Economic Consequences," *The Accounting Review* (October 1983), pp. 706-732.

LATANÉ, H., and C. JONES, "Standardized Unexpected Earnings: 1971-77," *Journal of Finance* (June 1979), pp. 717-724.

LEFTWICH, R., "Evidence of the Impact of Mandatory Changes in Accounting Principles on Corporate Loan Agreements," *Journal of Accounting and Economics* (March 1981), pp. 3-36.

LEROY, S., "Risk Aversion and the Martingale Property of Stock Prices," *International Economic Review* (June 1973), pp. 436-446.

_____ , "Efficient Capital Markets: Comment," *Journal of Finance* (March 1976), pp. 139-141.

_____ , and C. LA CIVITA, "Risk Aversion and the Dispersion of Asset Prices," *Journal of Business* (October 1981), pp. 535-547.

_____ , and R. PORTER, "The Present-Value Relation: Tests Based on Implied Variance Bounds," *Econometrica* (May 1981), pp. 555-574.

LEV, B., "The Impact of Accounting Regulation on the Stock Market: The Case of Oil and Gas Companies," *The Accounting Review* (July 1979), pp. 485-503.

LEVY, H., "Equilibrium in an Imperfect Market: A Constraint on the Number of Securities in the Portfolio," *American Economic Review* (September 1978), pp. 643-658.

LEVY, R., "Random Walks: Reality or Myth," *Financial Analysts Journal* (November-December 1967), pp. 69-76.

LINTNER, J., "The Valuation of Risky Assets and the Selection of Risky Investments in Stock Portfolios and Capital Budgets," *Review of Economics and Statistics* (February 1965), pp. 13-37. (a)

_____ , "Security Prices, Risk and Maximal Gains from Diversification," *Journal of Finance* (December 1965), pp. 587-616. (b)

_____ , "The Aggregation of Investor's Diverse Judgments and

Preferences in Purely Competitive Security Markets," *Journal of Financial and Quantitative Analysis* (December 1969), pp. 347–400.

LORIE, J., and M. HAMILTON, *The Stock Market: Theories and Evidence.* Homewood, Ill.: Richard D. Irwin, 1973.

———, and V. NIEDERHOFFER, "Predictive and Statistical Properties of Insider Training," *Journal of Law and Economics* (April 1968), pp. 35-53.

MALKIEL, B., and R. QUANDT, "The Supply of Money and Common Stock Prices, A Comment," *Journal of Finance* (September 1972), pp. 921-926.

MANASTER, S., and R. RENDLEMAN, "Option Prices as Predictors of Equilibrium Stock Prices," *Journal of Finance* (September 1982), pp. 1043-1058.

MANDELKER, G., "Risk and Return: The Case of Merging Firms," *Journal of Financial Economics* (December 1974), pp. 303-336.

MARKOWITZ, H., "Portfolio Selection," *Journal of Finance* (March 1952), pp. 77-91.

MAY, R., "The Influence of Quarterly Earnings Announcements on Investor Decision of Reflected in Common Stock Price Changes," *Journal of Accounting Research, Supplement* (1971), pp. 119-163.

———, and G. SUNDEM, "Cost of Information and Security Prices: Market Association Tests for Accounting Policy Decisions," *The Accounting Review* (January 1973), pp. 80-94.

MAYERS, D., "Nonmarketable Assets and the Determination of Capital Asset Prices in the Absence of a Riskless Asset," *Journal of Business* (April 1973), pp. 258-267.

———, and E. RICE, "Measuring Portfolio Performance and the Empirical Content of Asset Pricing Models," *Journal of Financial Economics* (March 1979), pp. 3-28.

MAYSHAR, J., "Transaction Costs and the Pricing of Assets," *Journal of Finance* (June 1981), pp. 583-598.

MCDONALD, J., and A. FISHER, "New Issue Stock Price Behavior," *Journal of Finance* (March 1972), pp. 97-102.

MERTON, R., "An Intertemporal Capital Asset Pricing Model," *Econometrica* (September 1973), pp. 867-888.

MICHENER, R., "Variance Bounds in a Simple Model of Asset Pricing," *Journal of Political Economics* (February 1982), pp. 166-175.

MILLER, E., "Risk, Undertainty, and Divergence of Opinion," *Journal of Finance* (September 1977), pp. 1151-1168.

MILLER, M., and F. MODIGLIANI, "Dividend Policy, Growth and the Valuation of Shares," *Journal of Business* (October 1961), pp. 411-433.

———, and M. SCHOLES, "Rates of Return in Relation to Risk: A Re-examination of Some Recent Findings." In M. Jensen, ed., *Studies in the Theory of Capital Markets.* New York: Praeger, 1972.

——, and M. SCHOLES, "Dividends and Taxes," *Journal of Financial Economics* (December 1978), pp. 333-354.

MLYNARCZYK, F., "An Empirical Study of Accounting Methods and Stock Prices," *Journal of Accounting Research, Supplement* (1969), pp. 63-81.

MOORE, A., "Some Characteristics of Changes in Common Stock Prices," in Paul Cootner, ed., *The Random Character of Stock Market Prices*. Cambridge, Mass.: M.I.T. Press, 1964, pp. 139-161.

MORSE, D., "Asymmetrical Information in Securities Markets and Trading Volume," *Journal of Financial and Quantitative Analysis* (December 1980). pp. 1129-1148.

——, "Price and Trading Volume Reaction Surrounding Earnings Announcements: A Closer Examination," *Journal of Accounting Research* (Autumn 1981), pp. 374-383.

MOSSIN, J., "Equilibrium in a Capital Asset Market," *Econometrica* (October 1966), pp. 768-783.

NICHOLS, W., and S. BROWN, "Assimilating Earnings and Split Information: Is the Capital Market Becoming More Efficient?" *Journal of Financial Economics* (September 1981), pp. 309-316.

NOREEN, E., and J. SEPE, "Market Reactions to Accounting Policy Deliberations: The Inflation Accounting Case," *The Accounting Review* (April 1981), pp. 253-269.

O'DONNELL, J., "Relationships Between Reported Earnings and Stock Prices in the Electric Utility Industry," *The Accounting Review* (January 1965), pp. 135-143.

——, "Further Observations on Reported Earnings and Stock Prices," *The Accounting Review* (July 1968), pp. 549-553.

OPPENHEIMER, H., and G. SCHLARBAUM, "Investing with Ben Graham: An Ex Ante Test of the Efficient Markets Hypothesis," *Journal of Financial and Quantitative Analysis* (September 1981), pp. 341-360.

OSBORNE, M., "Brownian Motion in the Stock Market," *Operations Research* (March-April 1959), pp. 145-173.

PATELL, J., and M. WOLFSON, "Anticipated Information Releases Reflected in Call Option Prices," *Journal of Accounting and Economics* (August 1979), pp. 117-140.

——, and M. WOLFSON, "The Ex Ante and Ex Post Price Effects of Quarterly Earnings Announcements Reflected in Option and Stock Prices," *Journal of Accounting Research* (Autumn 1981) pp. 434-458.

PENMAN, S., "Insider Trading and the Dissemination of Firms' Forecast Information," *Journal of Business* (October 1982), pp. 479-504.

PESANDO, J., "The Supply of Money and Common Stock Prices: Further Observations of the Econometric Evidence," *Journal of Finance* (June 1974), pp. 909-922.

PETIT, R., "Dividend Announcements, Security Performance and Capital Market Efficiency," *Journal of Finance* (December 1972), pp. 993-1007.

PLOTT, C., and S. SUNDER, "Efficiency of Experimental Security Markets with Insider Information: An Application of Rational-Expectations Models," *Journal of Political Economy* (August 1982), pp. 663–698.

RADNER, R., "Rational Expectations Equilibrium: Generic Existence and the Information Revealed by Prices," *Econometrica* (May 1979), pp. 655–678.

REINGANUM, M., "The Arbitrage Pricing Theory: Some Empirical Results," *Journal of Finance* (May 1981), pp. 313–322. (a)

_____ , "A New Empirical Perspective on the CAPM," *Journal of Financial and Quantitative Analysis* (November 1981), pp. 439–462. (b)

_____ , "Misspecification of Capital Asset Pricing: Empirical Anomalies Based on Earnings' Yields and Market Values," *Journal of Financial Economics* (March 1981), pp. 19–46. (c)

_____ , "A Direct Test of Roll's Conjecture on the Firm Size Effect," *Journal of Finance* (March 1982), pp. 27–35.

_____ , "The Anomalous Stock Market Behavior of Small Firms in January: Empirical Tests for Tax-Loss Selling Effects," *Journal of Financial Economics* (June 1983), pp. 89–104.

RENDLEMAN, R., C. JONES, and H. LATANE, "Empirical Anomalies Based on Unexpected Earnings and the Importance of Risk Adjustments," *Journal of Financial Economics* (November 1982), pp. 269–287.

RICKS, W., "The Market's Response to the 1974 LIFO Adoptions," *Journal of Accounting Research* (Autumn 1982), pp. 367–387.

RO, B., "The Adjustment of Security Returns to the Disclosure of Replacement Cost Accounting Information," *Journal of Accounting and Economics* (August 1980), pp. 159–189.

ROBERTS H., "Stock Market 'Patterns' and Financial Analysis: Methodological Suggestions," *Journal of Finance* (March 1959), pp. 1–10.

ROLL, R., "A Critique of the Asset Pricing Theory's Tests. Part I: On Past and Potential Testability of the Theory," *Journal of Financial Economics* (March 1977), pp. 129–179.

_____ , "A Possible Explanation of the Small Firm Effect," *Journal of Finance* (September 1981), pp. 879–888.

_____ , "The Turn of the Year Effect and the Return Premia of Small Firms," *Journal of Portfolio Management* (Winter 1983), pp. 18–28.

_____ , and S. ROSS, "An Empirical Investigation of the Arbitrage Pricing Theory," *Journal of Finance* (December 1980), pp. 1073–1103.

ROSENBERG, B., and A. RUDD, "Factor Related and Specific Returns of Common Stocks: Serial Correlation and Market Efficiency," *Journal of Finance* (May 1982), pp. 543–554.

ROSS, S., "The Arbitrage Theory of Capital Asset Pricing," *Journal of Economic Theory*, (December 1976), pp. 341–360.

_____ , "Return, Risk and Arbitrage." in I. Friend and J. Bicksler, eds., *Risk and Return in Finance*. Cambridge, Mass.: Ballinger, 1977.

———, "The Current Status of the Capital Asset Pricing Model," *Journal of Finance* (June 1978), pp. 885–901.

ROZEFF, M., "Money and Stock Prices: Market Efficiency and the Lag in effect of Monetary Policy," *Journal of Financial Economics* (September 1974), pp. 245–302.

———, and W. KINNEY, "Capital Market Seasonality: The Case of Stock Returns," *Journal of Financial Economics* (October 1976), pp. 379–402.

RUBINSTEIN, M., "Securities Market Efficiency in an Arrow-Debreu Economy," *American Economic Review* (December 1975), pp. 812–824.

SAMUELSON, P., "Proof That Properly Anticipated Prices Fluctuate Randomly," *Industrial Management Review* (Spring 1965), pp. 41–49.

SCHLARBAUM, G., W. LEWELLEN, and R. LEASE, "The Common Stock Portfolio Performance Record of Individual Investors: 1964–70," *Journal of Finance* (May 1978), pp. 429–442.

SCHOLES, M., "The Market for Securities: Substitution versus Price Pressure and the Effects of Information Share Prices," *Journal of Business* (April 1972), pp. 179–211.

———, and J. WILLIAMS, "Estimating Betas from Nonsynchronous Data," *Journal of Financial Economics* (December 1977), pp. 309–328.

SCHULTZ, P., "Transaction Costs and the Small Firm Effect: A Comment," *Journal of Financial Economics* (June 1983), pp. 81–88.

SCHWARTZ, R., and D. WHITCOMB, "The Time-Variance Relationship Evidence on Autocorrelation in Common Stock Returns," *Journal of Finance* (March 1977), pp. 41–56. (a)

———, and D. WHITCOMB, "Evidence on the Presence and Causes of Serial Correlation in Market Model Residuals," *Journal of Financial and Quantitative Analysis* (June 1977), pp. 291–314. (b)

SCHWERT, G., "The Adjustment of Stock Prices to Information About Inflation," *Journal of Finance* (March 1981), pp. 15–30.

SHANKEN, J., "The Arbitrage Pricing Theory: Is It Testable?" *Journal of Finance* (December 1982), pp. 1129–1140.

SHARPE, W., "A Simplified Model of Portfolio Analysis," *Management Science* (January 1963), pp. 277–293.

———, "Capital Asset Prices: A Theory of Market Equilibrium Under Conditions of Risk," *Journal of Finance* (September 1964), pp. 425–442.

———, "Mutual Fund Performance," *Journal of Business* (January 1966), pp. 119–138.

SHILLER, R., "Do Stock Prices Move Too Much to Be Justified by Subsequent Changes in Dividends?" *American Economic Review* (June 1981), pp. 421–436. (a)

———, "The Use of Volatility Measures in Assessing Market Efficiency," *Journal of Finance* (May 1981), pp. 291–303. (b)

SMITH, A., "The SEC 'Reversal' of FASB Statement No. 19: An

Investigation of Information Effects," *Journal of Accounting Research, Supplement* (1981) pp. 174-211.

STAMBAUGH, R., "On the Exclusion of Assets from Tests of the Two-Parameter Model: A Sensitivity Analysis," *Journal of Financial Economics* (November 1982), pp. 237-268.

STOLL, H., and R. WHALEY, "Transaction Costs and the Small Firm Effect," *Journal of Financial Economics* (June 1983), pp. 57-79.

SUNDER, S., "Relationship Between Accounting Changes and Stock Prices: Problems of Measurement and Some Empirical Evidence," *Supplement to the Journal of Accounting Research* (1973), pp. 1-45.

_____ , "Stock Price and Risk Related to Accounting Changes in Inventory Valuation," *The Accounting Review* (April 1975), pp. 305-315.

THOMPSON, R., "The Information Content of Discounts and Premiums on Closed-End Fund Shares," *Journal of Financial Economics* (June/September 1978), pp. 151-186.

VIGELAND, R., "The Market Reaction to Statement of Financial Accounting Standards No. 2," *The Accounting Review* (April 1981), pp. 309-325.

WATTS, R., "Systematic 'Abnormal' Returns After Quarterly Earnings Announcement," *Journal of Financial Economics* (June/September 1978), pp. 127-150.

_____ , and J. ZIMMERMAN, "Towards a Positive Theory of the Determination of Accounting Standards," *The Accounting Review* (January 1978), pp. 112-134.

_____ , and J. ZIMMERMAN, "On the Irrelevance of Replacement Cost Disclosures for Security Prices," *Journal of Accounting and Economics* (August 1980), pp. 95-106.

WAUD, R., "Public Interpretation of Federal Reserve Discount Rate Changes: Evidence on the 'Announcement Effect,'" *Econometrica* (March 1970), pp. 231-250.

WELLES, C., "The Beta Revolution: Learning to Live with Risk," *Institutional Investor* (September 1971), pp. 21-64.

WILLIAMS, J., "Capital Asset Prices with Heterogeneous Beliefs," *Journal of Financial Economics* (November 1977), pp. 219-239.

WOOLRIDGE, R., "Ex-Date Stock Price Adjustment to Stock Dividends: A Note," *Journal of Finance* (March 1983), pp. 247-255.

APPENDIX A

Expectation, Variance, Covariance, and Skewness

Each of these terms—expectation, variance, covariance, and skewness—finds extensive use in the efficient market literature. For this reason, the reader must understand them at least at an intuitive level before attempting the mathematical statement of the efficient market hypothesis (EMH) in Appendix B. We have also occasionally referred to these notions in parenthetical remarks or footnotes to be more precise about a point in the text.

A.1 EXPECTATION

Suppose you engage in a game with someone in which you win one dollar if the flip of a coin results in a head, and you lose a dollar if the flip of the coin results in a tail. The coin, we assume, has a 50-50 chance of turning up heads. The outcome of the flip is a random event, so the payment (receipt) of the money is a random variable. The expectation of this game is defined to be equal to the product of what you can win multiplied by the probability of winning, less the product of what you can lose multiplied by the probability of losing. In the example $\$1(\frac{1}{2}) - \$1(\frac{1}{2}) = \$0$.

This was an even or "fair" game. No one had an advantage. Whenever the game is a fair game, the expectation will be zero. Note that you do not receive the expectation on any one play. On a single play you either win or lose one dollar. But on two plays you would *expect*, on the average, to win once and lose once, a net of zero over the two plays. In this sense the concept of an expectation is a long-run average notion. Indeed, we often refer to the expected return as the average or mean return.

For a second example, suppose the dollar bet is resolved by the roll of an honest die where you win on the numbers 1 through 4 inclusive. The expectation of this new game is $\$1(\%) - \$1(\%) = \$2/6 = \$0.33$. The positive expectation indicates the game is in your favor as far as the monetary amount is concerned.

Formally, we express the expectation using the letter E and place the variable (winnings) in parentheses. Thus, if we let x_i be the amount won, for the second example, we have

$$\text{Expected Value} = \$1(\%) + (-\$1)(\%)$$
$$E(\tilde{X}) = x_1 \cdot p(x_1) + x_2 \cdot p(x_2)$$
$\tilde{X} \equiv$ the amount of money received. The tilde ($\sim$) signifies that this amount is a random variable

where

$$x_1 \equiv x_{\text{win}} \equiv \text{the amount to be won}$$
$$x_2 \equiv x_{\text{lose}} \equiv \text{the amount to be lost}$$
$$p(x_1) \equiv p(x_{\text{win}}) \equiv \text{the probability of winning}$$

and

$$p(x_2) \equiv p(x_{\text{lose}}) \equiv \text{the probability of losing.}$$

In the most general notational form, we write

$$E(\tilde{X}) = \sum_i x_i \cdot p(x_i). \tag{A1}$$

A.2 VARIANCE

We observed that in one play of either of the games described in the previous section the expected value would not be the result. Hence, in the second example, the expectation is $\$0.33$. Yet on a single play the result is either a dollar won or a dollar lost. The variance is one measure of the dispersion of the actual returns about the mean or expected return. More precisely, it measures the average squared deviation of the actual returns around the expectation. Each possible deviation is weighted by its likelihood. For the second example, we have

$$\text{Variance} = (1 - .33)^2 \, (\tfrac{4}{6}) + (-1 - .33)^2 \, (\tfrac{2}{6})$$
$$\text{Var} \, (\tilde{X}) = (.67)^2 \, (\tfrac{4}{6}) + (-1.33)^2 \, (\tfrac{2}{6})$$
$$\sigma^2 \, (\tilde{X}) = 0.89.$$

The use of the variance as a measure of the dispersion of the returns implicitly assumes that the effect of variability is best captured by the square of the difference between a particular return and the expectation. Thus, a return that is twice as far removed from the expectation as some other return is four times as important in measuring the impact of the variability of the return.

Using general notation, the variance is written as

$$\sigma^2(\tilde{X}) = E([\tilde{X} - E(\tilde{X})]^2$$
$$= \sum_i [x_i - E(\tilde{X})]^2 \cdot p(x_i) \qquad \text{(A2)}$$

The square root of the variance is the standard deviation and is denoted by the sumbol $\sigma(\tilde{X})$.

The reader will note that we have considered only variables that take on measurable probabilities at discrete points. This is done on purpose, since only discrete variables are required to understand the material in this book. Formulas for continuous variables are similar to (A1) and (A2) except that (1) an integration sign replaces the summation symbol and (2) the expression $f(x)dx$ replaces $p(x_i)$ to caution the reader that a probability density function, which is required for a continuous variable, is being used.

A.3 COVARIANCE

The prefix "co-" signifies together or joint. A covariance relates to two variables rather than just one. It measures how the two variables vary in a joint sense: Do they rise together, fall together, or move with no apparent joint relationship?

We can again use a simple gambling analogy to illustrate this concept. Suppose, based on the roll of a die, you receive from two other players (or, alternatively, make to two other players) the following dollar payments:

Event	Result of Die	Probability	Received from (Paid to) Player X	Received from (Paid to) Player Y
1	1 or 2	$\tfrac{1}{3}$	+$1	−$1
2	3 or 4	$\tfrac{1}{3}$	0	0
3	5 or 6	$\tfrac{1}{3}$	−$1	+$1

The minus sign indicates a payment made, the plus sign a payment received.

In this case the payments to players X and Y move opposite to one another. They vary inversely rather than directly. When the payment to one player is high, the payment to the other is low, and vice versa. The covariance is measured as the sum of several products. Each of these is the product of the differences of the payoffs from their own expectation for each variable under each event.

$$\text{Covariance} = [x_1 - E(\tilde{X})]\,[y_1 - E(\tilde{Y})] \cdot p(x_1, y_1)$$
$$+ [x_2 - E(\tilde{X})]\,[y_2 - E(\tilde{Y})] \cdot p(x_2, y_2)$$
$$+ [x_3 - E(\tilde{X})]\,[y_3 - E(\tilde{Y})] \cdot p(x_3, y_3)$$
$$\text{Cov}\,(\tilde{X}, \tilde{Y}) = [1 - 0]\,[-1 - 0] \cdot \tfrac{1}{3} + [0 - 0]\,[0 - 0] \cdot \tfrac{1}{3}$$
$$+ [-1 - 0]\,[1 - 0] \cdot \tfrac{1}{3}$$
$$\sigma(\tilde{X}, \tilde{Y}) = -\tfrac{1}{3} + 0 - \tfrac{1}{3} = -\tfrac{2}{3}$$

The negative value reflects the inverse relationship.

The symbol $p(x_i, y_i)$ stands for the joint probability that x and y take on the indicated values simultaneously. Thus, the probability that both payoffs are zero at the same time, $p(x = 0, y = 0) = p(x_2, y_2)$, is the probability the die shows a 3 or a 4. This occurs one-third of the time. Hence $p(x_2, y_2) = \tfrac{1}{3}$.

In general terms, we may write the covariance as

$$\sigma(\tilde{X}, \tilde{Y}) = E([\tilde{X} - E(\tilde{X})] \cdot [\tilde{Y} - E(Y)]$$
$$= \sum_i [x_i - E(\tilde{X})] \cdot [y_i - E(\tilde{Y})] \cdot p(x_i, y_i). \qquad \text{(A3)}$$

To illustrate the effect on the covariance when the variables move together, suppose the payoffs received from Y were \$1 for a "1" or "2" on the die, 0 for a "3" or "4," and −\$1 for a "5" or "6". The payoffs from X remain unchanged. Then

$$\sigma(\tilde{X}, \tilde{Y}) = [1 - 0]\,[1 - 0] \cdot \tfrac{1}{3} + [0 - 0]\,[0 - 0] \cdot \tfrac{1}{3}$$
$$+ [-1 - 0]\,[-1 - 0] \cdot \tfrac{1}{3}$$
$$= \tfrac{2}{3}$$

In this case the positive value reflects the direct relationship. When there is little or no relationship between the movement of two variables, the covariance is close to zero. This is illustrated by the following set of values.

x_i	y_i	$p(x_i, y_i)$
2	−1	$\tfrac{1}{4}$
2	+1	$\tfrac{1}{4}$
−2	−1	$\tfrac{1}{4}$
−2	+1	$\tfrac{1}{4}$

The expected values of both X and Y are zero using formula (A1). The covariance is given by

$$\sigma(\tilde{X}, \tilde{Y}) = [2 - 0][-1 - 0] \cdot \frac{1}{4} + [2 - 0][1 - 0] \cdot \frac{1}{4}$$
$$+ [-2 - 0][-1 - 0] \cdot \frac{1}{4} + [-2 - 0][1 - 0] \cdot \frac{1}{4}$$
$$= -\frac{1}{2} + \frac{1}{2} + \frac{1}{2} - \frac{1}{2}$$
$$= 0$$

The three cases we have discussed in regard to the covariance are illustrated in Figure A-1. The positive relationship $\sigma(\tilde{X}, \tilde{Y}) > 0$ is suggested by the solid line sloping upward to the right. The negative relationship $\sigma(\tilde{X}, \tilde{Y}) < 0$ is illustrated by the dashed line sloping downward to the right. The lack of a definite relationship is indicated by the dotted boxlike figure involving the points $(2, -1)$, $(2, +1)$, $(-2, -1)$ and $(-2, +1)$.

In general, then, if two variables tend to move together, their covariance will be positive. If they tend to move inversely with one another, their covariance will be negative. And if such movements tend to cancel out, their covariance will be near zero.

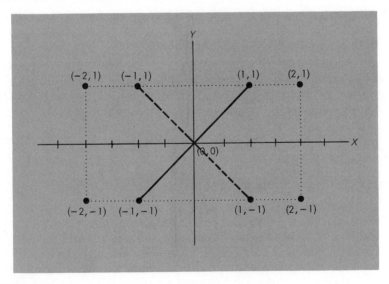

FIGURE A-1

Illustration of three separate types of covariance.

A.4 SKEWNESS

A set of data can usually be described by a number of measures. One measure that describes the nonsymmetrical characteristics of a set of data is called skewness. The histogram in Figure A-2 illustrates a symmetrical distribution while that in Figure A-3 illustrates a distribution that is skewed to the right.

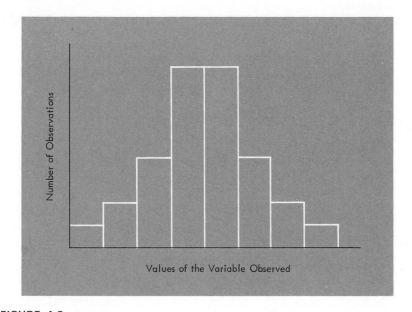

FIGURE A-2

A symmetrical distribution.

FIGURE A-3

Distribution skewed to the right.

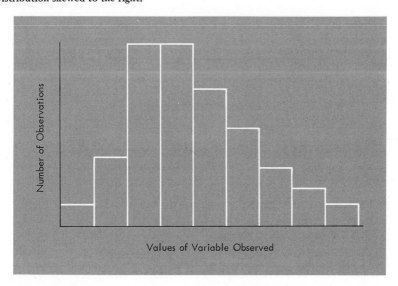

There are several ways of measuring the skewness of the outcomes of a random variable. One simple measure is calculated using the formula:

$$\text{Skewness} = \frac{E([\tilde{X} - E(\tilde{X})]^3)}{[\sigma(\tilde{X})]^3}$$

A symmetrical distribution will have a zero skewness, while a distribution skewed to the right (left) will have a positive (negative) skewness measure. Calculation of the skewness for each of the gambles described in Section A.1 yields

	Game 1	Game 2
Expectation, $E(\tilde{X})$	$0	$0.33
Standard deviation, $\sigma(\tilde{X})$	1.0	0.943
Skewness	0	−0.70

APPENDIX B

A Mathematical Statement of the Efficient Market Hypothesis and Related Models

The purpose of this appendix is to present a concise mathematical representation of the various models that have found extensive use in the research into efficient markets. Reference to several of these models is made at various places in the text.

B.1 THE EXPECTED RETURNS MODEL

The essence of the efficient market hypothesis (EMH) is stated mathematically in the expected returns model. The model, suggested by Fama [1970], is given by

$$Z_{i, t+1} = r_{i, t+1} - E[\tilde{r}_{i, t+1} \mid \phi_t] \qquad (B1)$$

with

$$E[\tilde{Z}_{i, t+1} \mid \phi_t] = 0 \qquad (B2)$$

where $Z_{i, t+1}$ is the unexpected (or excess) return for security i in period $t+1$, the difference between the observed return, $r_{i, t+1}$, and the expected return based on the information set ϕ_t. The expected return term obtains its value from some theory of expected returns beyond the expected return model; for example, this value could be

113

based on the capital asset pricing model (CAPM) [Sharpe, 1964] to be described later in this appendix.

By defining information in different ways, Fama [1970] suggests three levels of market efficiency: the weak, the semistrong, and the strong form. The weak form of the hypothesis states that equilibrium prices reflect fully any information contained in the sequence of historical prices. In its semistrong form, the hypothesis is extended to incorporate all publicly available information and hence is of particular interest to accountants because financial statements are contained in the information set. The strong form adds inside information. This information specification is represented in the model by the ϕ_t term and, as the subscript denotes, is time specific.

The various empirical tests of the EMH described in Chapters 3 and 4 have grown out of the implications that can be derived from the mathematical specifications given in equations (B1) and (B2).

B.2 THE CAPITAL ASSET PRICING MODEL

The EMH as expressed by the expected returns model and summarized by equations (B1) and (B2) requires the use of expected returns in the expectation term of the first equation. Further, if an efficient market is a reasonably accurate hypothesis, then securities are (approximately) properly priced relative to each other. To specify appropriate relationships between individual stocks' expected returns in order to establish specific stock prices, we can use the capital asset pricing model (CAPM) developed by Sharpe [1964], Lintner [February 1965], and Mossin [1966]. This model may be expressed mathematically as

$$E(\tilde{r}_{it}) = r_{ft} + [E(\tilde{r}_{mt}) - r_{ft}] \frac{\sigma(\tilde{r}_{it}, \tilde{r}_{mt})}{\sigma^2(\tilde{r}_{mt})} \tag{B3}$$

where

$E(\tilde{r}_{it}) \equiv$ the expected return of security i in period t

$r_{ft} \equiv$ the return on a riskless asset in period t

$E(\tilde{r}_{mt}) \equiv$ the expected return on the market portfolio in period t

$\sigma(\tilde{r}_{it}, \tilde{r}_{mt}) \equiv$ the covariance between $\tilde{r}_{it}$ and $\tilde{r}_{mt}$ (see Appendix A for a discussion of covariance)

$\sigma^2(\tilde{r}_{mt}) \equiv$ the variance of the return on the market portfolio

This model embodies the following assumptions:

1. Investors are risk-averse, single-period, expected-utility-of-terminal-wealth maximizers who select their holdings of securities on the basis of the mean and variance of the probability distribution of returns.
2. Investors can borrow or lend unlimited amounts at a common and exogenously determined riskless rate (r_{ft}).
3. Investors have homogeneous expectations; that is, they agree about the means, variances, and covariances of returns among all securities.
4. Perfect capital markets exist; that is, investors are price takers. There are no taxes or transactions costs, and all investors have equal and costless access to information.
5. The quantities of securities are fixed.

Thus the capital asset pricing model asserts that the only variable that determines the differences in expected returns is the risk coefficient given by

$$\lambda_i = \frac{\sigma(\tilde{r}_{it}, \tilde{r}_{mt})}{\sigma^2(\tilde{r}_{mt})} \tag{B4}$$

and that the relationship between this risk coefficient and expected return is linear. The risk coefficient is the ratio of the covariance between the particular securities return and the market, to the variance of the market. When the security's return and the market move together, then $\sigma(\tilde{r}_{it}, \tilde{r}_{mt})$ will be positive. The closer the covariability, the larger the risk measure.

The CAPM is neutral concerning the process that generates security prices. However, some such assumption is generally necessary in order to estimate the expected return series employed in tests of the efficient market using the expected returns model. To provide for this need the market model developed by Markowitz [1952] and Sharpe [1963] has been extensively used.

B.2.1 The Market Model

The market model developed in conjunction with portfolio theory states that security returns are a linear function of a general market factor. The relationship can be written as

$$\tilde{r}_{it} = a_i + \beta_i \tilde{R}_{mt} + \tilde{\mu}_{it} \tag{B5}$$

where

$$E(\tilde{\mu}_{it}) = 0$$

$$\sigma(\tilde{R}_{mt}, \tilde{\mu}_{it}) = 0$$

$$\sigma(\tilde{\mu}_{it}, \tilde{\mu}_{jt}) = 0$$

$\tilde{r}_{it} \equiv$ return on security i in period t

$\tilde{R}_{mt} \equiv$ general market factor in period t

$\tilde{\mu}_{it} \equiv$ the stochastic portion of the individualistic factor representing the part of security i's return, which is independent of $\tilde{R}_{mt}$

$a_i, \beta_i \equiv$ intercept and slope, respectively, of the linear relationship

Basically, the model states that the stochastic portion of a security's return can be separated into a systematic component, represented by $\beta_i \tilde{R}_{mt}$, and an individualistic component, $\tilde{\mu}_{it}$.

The general market factor in equation (B5) is designed to reflect general market and economic conditions that are related to the returns on a particular security. This is a different notion from the return on the market portfolio in the CAPM given by $\tilde{r}_{mt}$. For this reason different symbols are used to represent these two similar but distinct concepts.

The only assumption needed for the market model is the first assumption of the CAPM, namely, that investors are risk-averse, single-period, expected-utility-of-terminal-wealth maximizers who select their holdings of securities on the basis of the mean and variance of the distribution of returns.[1] In empirical research studies, estimates of a_i and β_i for each security are obtained from past data using ordinary least squares regression.

The market model hypothesizes a stochastic process that generates security returns. It is consistent with several alternate equilibrium pricing models of which the Lintner, Sharpe, and Mossin models are only a few. Acceptance of the market model does not compel acceptance of the Lintner-Sharpe-Mossin CAPM, or vice versa. However, the links between these two models through the expected return model suggest the value to be obtained by connecting them.

The discussion of the two models and the assumptions behind them given here is intentionally brief. A more extensive coverage is available in Beaver [1972]. Also, a nontechnical discussion of beta (β_i) is given by Welles [1971].

B.3 THE ARBITRAGE PRICING MODEL

A central notion of modern portfolio theory is that the covariability of an asset's return with the return on other assets, rather than its total variability, is important to a risk-averse investor. This

---

[1] The risk-averse assumption based on the mean-variance argument is consistent with maximizing the expected utility of terminal wealth only under severely restrictive conditions. Few decreasingly risk-averse utility functions can be integrated with the normal probability density function.

is reflected in equations (B3 and B4). Ross's [1976] primary contribution was to show that this same notion could be transformed into a theory of asset pricing with implications similar to those implied by equation (B4).

While the development of the CAPM requires several specific and technical assumptions, the APM relies on a many-asset security market. The market portfolio plays no role in the APM. Instead, it is the covariability of an asset's return with those factors that systematically influence the return on most assets that is reflected in the expected return relation.

The APM is an assumed linear relation relationship between the random return on asset i in period t (R_{it}) and its expected return (E_{it}) plus a set of common factors denoted by X_{jt} ($j = 1, \ldots, n$), each with zero mean. More formally

$$R_{it} = E_{it} + b_{i1}X_{it} + b_{i2}X_{2t} + \cdots + b_{in}X_{nt} + \mu_{it} \qquad (B6)$$

From a factor analytic viewpoint, the b_{ij}'s are the factor loadings on the common factors. Factor analytic techniques are used to fit the model. The researcher has the task of selecting the variables to use as the common factors in the model and of interpreting the economic meaning of these factors.

The model acts as a multifactor, ex post model of security returns. It allows one to measure unexpected returns as a linear function of the common factors.

B.4 THE ABNORMAL PERFORMANCE INDEX (API)

Accounting researchers have used the models discussed already to examine empirically the effects of accounting numbers. One of the more imaginative developments in this approach was the development of the abnormal performance index (API) by Ball and Brown [1968] to study the association between unexpected changes in accounting earnings and unexpected changes in prices.

A form of the market model with coefficients based on a time series regression is used to form earnings expectations conditional on the observed ex post value of a market earnings factor. The residual, call it e_{it} for earnings residual, is the earnings forecast error, assuming the model is an appropriate expression of expectations. The signs of the earnings forecast errors for the various securities are used to form portfolios. Simultaneously, the market model is also used to compute a price residual, the unexpected change in price μ_{it}, again conditional on the observed ex post market price. The unexpected price changes are aggregated (for the portfolios formed using the sign of the earnings forecast error) using the relationship

$$\text{API} = \frac{1}{N} \cdot \sum_{i}^{N} \prod_{t}^{T} (1 + \mu_{it}) - 1 \qquad (B7)$$

$T \equiv$ number of time periods: $t = 1, 2, \dots, T$

$N \equiv$ number of securities: $i = 1, 2, \dots, N$

$\mu_{it} \equiv$ individualistic component of r_{it} or, alternately, the forecast error

The API traces out the value of a dollar invested in equal amounts in each security in the portfolio from time t up to time T. At time T the earnings number is assumed to be made public.

As Beaver [1972] notes, the API has an appealing intuitive interpretation. It represents one measure of the value of the information contained in the earnings number (actually the sign of the earnings forecast error) T months prior to the release of the earnings number. In this sense the API concept has some aspects of similarity to the notion of perfect information as the concept is used in decision theory. The analogy is not perfect, however, for the API is an ex post concept while the value of perfect information is an ex ante notion.

The API measures the return obtained from a specific and unusual investment strategy. The index assumes that information is obtained by the investor (in most studies) 12 months before it is public knowledge. The information received by the investor is a forecast of whether a firm's earnings will increase or decrease. The investor then adopts a long position (buying) in the firm's stock if the earnings change forecast is positive or a short position if the change forecasted is negative. The API measures the return obtained from this strategy. In calculating the value of the index, both the earnings expectation and the return obtained are adjusted for market change. Hence, the earnings change forecasted is the change over and above that due to the movement of earnings levels generally; it is the unexpected earnings change. Likewise, it is the unexpected return, the security's return after allowing for the effect on the firm's stock price of the overall market movement, that is used to measure the abnormal performance. The investor is assumed to know the sign of the unexpected earnings change and the methodology determines whether this allows the investor to make an unexpected (abnormal) return.

The API implies a portfolio in which an equal dollar investment is made in each security at the start of the analysis and this investment is not altered over the period studied. An alternative formulation advanced by Fama, Fisher, Jensen, and Roll [1969] assumes a portfolio in which the investment in each security is adjusted through transactions so that an equal dollar investment for each security holds at the start of each period. This is a rebalancing approach. The Fama formulation is called the cumulative average residual.

The transactions implied by the Fama approach, an equal dollar investment in each security at the start of each period, make it less appealing than the simple buy-and-hold strategy implicit to the API. On the other hand the API also has limitations. First it assumes that the systematic risk of the portfolio is constant, that is, in proportion to the initial weights reflected by $1/N$. But as the monthly weights change due to the buy-and-hold strategy, so does the systematic risk. Second, the API involves a number of cross-product terms due to the multiplicative nature of the formulation and may be dominated by these cross-product terms when measured over many time periods. Ball [1972] has observed that the API is misleading over long periods if the monthly abnormal performance is either consistently positive or consistently negative. For example, the reinvestment of initial negative performance at a negative rate produces a positive return that is difficult to interpret. Third, the API uses only a limited, but important, portion of the data contained in financial reports. Recent studies can be found that use either the Ball and Brown or the Fama method, depending on the merits of the two approaches as evaluated by the researcher.

Index

A

Abdel-Khalik, A., 42, 92

Abnormal performance index (API), 117-19

Abnormal returns:
  from accounting information, 41, 51-52, 55-63, 65-66
  EMH tests and, 28-42, 69
  in fair game concept, 83-85, 88, 89
  from mutual funds, 40-41
  pricing model adequacy and, 69, 78, 80
  See also Risk-adjusted returns

Accounting announcements, 48-49, 51-59, 88
  tests of returns following, 55-58

Accounting changes, 49, 60-67

Accounting changes, discretionary, 49, 61, 65-66

Accounting changes, mandatory, 61-65

Accounting disclosure increase, 49, 61-62

Accounting (earnings) numbers, 48-49, 51, 55-58, 64

Accounting information, 48-67, 86-91
  securities markets and, 3-4, 39, 48, 51-55, 66
  See also Information; Public information

Accounting methods, 39, 49, 51-59, 86-87

Accounting option constraints, 61, 63-65

Accounting practice, 86-88

Accounting principles, changing, 58, 60-65, 87, 88

Accounting Principles Board (APB), 50

Accounting reports, 2, 31, 51
  issuing of, 49, 51, 52, 53
  market reactions to, 51-55
  mispricing of, 8
  security prices change and, 51-55, 86-88

Accounting research, 88-91, 117

Accounting theory, 86-88, 90